NORTH CAROLINA
LIGHTHOUSES

NORTH CAROLINA
LIGHTHOUSES
STORIES OF HISTORY AND HOPE

CHERYL SHELTON-ROBERTS AND BRUCE ROBERTS

Guilford, Connecticut

All photographs by Bruce Roberts unless otherwise noted.

Text design: Sheryl Kober
Layout: Mary Ballachino
Project manager: Ellen Urban

Library of Congress Cataloging-in-Publication Data
Shelton-Roberts, Cheryl, 1950-
  North Carolina lighthouses : stories of history and hope / Cheryl Shelton-Roberts and Bruce Roberts.
    p. cm.
  Includes bibliographical references and index.
  ISBN 978-0-7627-7351-0
1. Lighthouses—North Carolina—History. 2. Lighthouses—North Carolina—Pictorial works. 3. Seafaring life—North Carolina—History. I. Roberts, Bruce, 1930- II. Title.
  VK1024.N8S44 2011
  387.1'5509756—dc23
                                                                                            2011025692

Printed in the United States of America

10 9 8 7 6 5 4 3 2

CONTENTS

Cape Hatteras Lighthouse is one of North Carolina's most recognized lighthouses due to its height and distinctive black-and-white-spiraled daymark.

FOREWORD

Lighthouses call to us, not just from across the water but also from across time. Their primary purpose—to guide mariners—and their basic form—a structure with a light at the top—have changed little in more than 2,000 years.

—RAY JONES, THE LIGHTHOUSE ENCYCLOPEDIA

Lighthouses are symbols of a history mysterious and far removed—yet they capture the imagination like little else because they are still part of us. They are tangible. We can touch and be touched by them; see what they have seen.

An extraordinary history runs through the lighthouses that have watched over North Carolina's beautiful capes, sounds, and rivers for centuries—in part influenced by human history but just as much dictated by the furtive nature of this part of the world. The Outer Banks define our state's outermost edge, but it is often hard to tell exactly where solid land ends and open water begins. Watching waves pound on the beach, it becomes obvious the land has only a tenuous hold—but also that the ocean's grip on its own domain is slippery. The sandy isles and shallow waters create an enchanting and disorienting illusion, and they have taken a deadly toll for as long as sailors have plied these waters.

North Carolina's shore stretches an impressive 301 miles, and unlike other Eastern Seaboard states that trend gently northeastward, it thrusts far out into the Atlantic Ocean, slicing across our nation's vital north-south shipping lanes. A long broken peninsula that appears to be coming unglued, these low-slung barrier islands are at many points invisible from the mainland—adding to the disorientation. They poked their heads above water thousands of years ago; dynamic in the extreme, the Banks have "perplexed scientists for centuries," says coastal geologist Stanley Riggs.

To the east of the islands lie three sweeping capes and gigantic sandy shoals. Cape Fear's Frying Pan Shoals near Wilmington, Cape Lookout and its shoals near Morehead City, and the knobby-knee of Cape Hatteras and Diamond Shoals at Buxton stretch underwater for miles. At Hatteras, sea captains had to choose between a longer and safer route east of the Gulf Stream or a quicker but riskier passage that made them roll the dice with the hidden shoals. Shipwrecks by the thousands litter the ocean bottom here.

North Carolina's lighthouse heritage begins, geographically at least, a few miles below the Virginia border. Rising above rolling sand dunes, the Currituck Beach Lighthouse was completed in 1875, the final link in lighting the state's entire coast. In the 1870s had come an extraordinary lighthouse-building boom—a series of projects so innovative that some historians have compared the overall effort to the U.S. space program. This bold undertaking gave North Carolina the best system of coastal towers and navigational lights in America.

To the south, near a key maritime passage called Oregon Inlet, stands the Bodie Island Lighthouse. A bit older than Currituck, it is the last of three lighthouses erected here. Further south, near where the island chain bends sharply to the southwest, the Cape Hatteras Lighthouse rises firmly rooted now half a mile from where it was built in 1870.

On Ocracoke Island endures the oldest North Carolina light still in operation, built in 1823. At the far southwestern corner of the Outer Banks, yet another brick giant illumines the night sky at Cape Lookout, constructed before the Civil War and a model for its brethren up the coast. The very oldest and the very newest lighthouses in the state are neighbors—Bald Head Island's 1817 "Old Baldy" and the 1958 Oak Island Light.

Like all of America's lighthouses, the story of North Carolina's beacons is about rising and falling fortunes. Not much needed after World War II with the advent of modern highways and sophisticated technologies, they fell into disrepair. They needed benefactors to care for them and a new sense of purpose, and happily many of these irreplaceable pieces of history have now regained their rightful places of honor.

In this book are the soul-stirring stories of North Carolina's lighthouses and the people who built them, were saved by them, cared for them, and now love them in a whole new way. It is a history of darkest danger, nearly unfathomable courage—and, above all, dazzling light.

—RAY JONES

INTRODUCTION

THE BEST OF THE AMERICAN CHARACTER

North Carolina has nine original, standing lighthouses, each one enjoyed by millions of residents and visitors for its individual characteristics. The 1870 Cape Hatteras Lighthouse is often accepted as the iconic representation of the state's majestic beacons. It is perhaps the most photographed, painted, visited, read about, and admired lighthouse in North America. It is the signature of our maritime history. It is a symbol of the U.S. Lighthouse Service and a memorial to the hundreds of caring professional men and women who made this dangerous coastline safer for adventuresome mariners. It is the signpost of the Graveyard of the Atlantic. It is the gnomon of the earth's sundial casting shadows on the places of rest for those who lost their lives while making journeys in these tricky waters. Further, it is undoubtedly one of the most recognized lighthouses in the world. East Carolina University geology professor and author, Dr. Stanley Riggs, likes to tell a story from the 1980s when he co-directed a United Nations program in Senegal, western Africa. During early introductions to local tribal leaders they asked Riggs where he was from. "I only got blank looks when I said that my home in North Carolina was just south of Washington, D.C. So, I drew a map of the East Coast in the sand with a very prominent Cape Hatteras Lighthouse. Their eyes lit up as they said something like 'Oh yes, we know Cape Hatteras!'"

Although Cape Hatteras is known for its towering height at 200 feet and its black and white spirals, it is only one of more than three dozen lighthouses, lightships, and sound/river lights that have graced the shores and inland sounds of the state over the past two centuries. At first, only a lantern hung on a post offered a humble light for local boaters headed home after a long day of fishing near Portsmouth and Ocracoke Islands during the 1700s.

After the nation organized into the United States, the federal government took over responsibility for building and maintaining lighthouses. The early

This extraordinary NASA satellite view defines the state's slender stretch of barrier islands and two of its three capes. Midpoint is Cape Hatteras like an elbow punching its way into the Atlantic Ocean and to the south is Cape Lookout. The milky auras along the shoreline and concentrated at the capes are notorious shoals that caused hundreds of vessels to wreck. Bones of old ships and lost lives lie beneath these areas. Photograph courtesy of NASA/Goddard Space Flight Center Scientific Visualization Studio

government tried to mark the dangerous shoals at the state's three capes as soon as possible to encourage trade. To warn of Frying Pan Shoals, the First Bald Head Island Lighthouse (1794), then also known as the Cape Fear Lighthouse, was the first federally funded light to adorn that river's edge in directing maritime traffic from the Atlantic Ocean into the Cape Fear River and onward to the great port of Wilmington in 1794. Next came a short, stone tower on Shell

Castle Island near Ocracoke and the first Cape Hatteras Lighthouse that were completed in 1803. Shell Castle marked Ocracoke Inlet that was, at the time, the state's only working inlet north of Cape Fear. It allowed vessels to enter the big sounds and head for mainland ports including Bath and Edenton. Setting a precedent, Hatteras had been built as a warning light, not a welcoming harbor light as had all its predecessors. There has never been a port at Hatteras—only mountains of shifting sand in the three-shoal formation known as Diamond Shoals at the heart of the Graveyard of the Atlantic. Cape Lookout warned of Lookout Shoals in 1812. Times and architecture changed, trained engineers became involved in building North Carolina's proud lighthouses, and the march of history and lighthouse work proceeded right up to the present.

The story of North Carolina's lighthouses is the essence of our nation's history. It is the story of a fledgling country struggling to gain independence and develop its own financial support. Lighthouses have always been considered buildings of humanity, the centers of communities each one crowned. These towers have known no prejudice except for a few years during the Civil War when several fell victim to it. They have served every mariner from every nation of the world. And the men and women who kept these lighthouses in top condition were focused on their jobs as public servants and most carried out their tasks with deep dedication. Lighthouses exemplify the best of the American character.

The first documented lighthouse was built in Alexandria, Egypt, in 300 BC. Destroyed after 1,500 years by an earthquake, "Pharos" was an enduring building estimated to have been more than 600 feet tall. It became the ideal for subsequent lighthouses in the world. The first lighthouse site in America was at Boston Harbor, Massachusetts, in 1716. Rebuilt in 1783, it still stands and, because of its historical significance, it is the only lighthouse that has a resident keeper due to an Act of Congress. Cape Hatteras embraces its own two-fold historical significance: It is the tallest brick lighthouse in the world, and its relocation 2,900 feet to the southwest in 1999 was a dynamic investment in preserving American maritime history.

For sea travelers, lighthouses demark the line between safety and danger. Although they are primarily made of masonry and mortar, lighthouses have come to represent far more than just the materials of which they are made, just as each of us represents far more than merely skin and bones. As technology has rendered lighthouses outmoded, they have endured as icons of beauty and wonder. Lighthouses are situated in alluring spots along our coastline where the ancient mariner in all of us is allowed to emerge.

THE MENACING BEAUTY OF THE ATLANTIC

North Carolina's coast stretches an impressive 301 miles between the borders of Virginia and South Carolina. This comprised more than one quarter of the entire coastline of the original thirteen English colonies, as noted by Outer Banks historian David Stick. It is modestly estimated that more than 600 ships met a watery grave off our shores. It has been said that if all shipwrecks were placed end to end, that one could walk for miles without touching water.

The lure of riches in new lands and the excitement of travel to exotic places have kept man constantly traveling the deep blue seas. Numbers of these wealth seekers and curious explorers found the shoreline of North Carolina including Captain Philip Amadas and Arthur Barlowe, who visited natives on north Core Banks between Cape Lookout and Cape Hatteras in 1585, sent by Sir Walter Raleigh in search of the perfect setting for the first English colony. They traveled clockwise tidal currents between America and Europe that had become a system of travel for experienced navigators. They began on the western European shores, swung south to the coast of Africa along the Canary Islands, on to the Caribbean to the southern shores of Florida. It was here that they rode the Gulf Stream toward Cape Hatteras. A ship's captain could then

Many wrecked on North Carolina's shores not knowing where in the world they were. Lighthouses often revealed the only clue as to a mariner's location due to the low, featureless islands that comprised the coastline.

choose to either head for Baltimore or New York or jump off at Cape Hatteras and continue to take advantage of the clockwise flow of the Gulf Stream back to Europe. Secrets about the Gulf Stream were held close to the cuff. Either a navigator learned its advantages by the school of hard knocks or information was shared only among the elite fraternity of experienced navigators.

Providence gave our good state a long and leggy shoreline ready for prime-time shipping industry; however, there were barriers—barrier islands, that is—that poked their heads above water several thousands of years ago as the result of an old drainage basin, according to geologist Stanley Riggs. And along with these leggy barriers, shallow sounds formed between them and the mainland, the results of built-up silt, sand, and mud that ran from voluminous rivers including the North, Pasquotank, Chowan, Roanoke, Tar, and Cape Fear and their tributaries throughout the state to the Atlantic Ocean. So, either ship captains negotiated the shoals on both sides of the barrier islands or they carried on to ports to the north or south of North Carolina. If they did, they were bypassing some of the finest lumber, naval stores, cotton, and tobacco to be had on the East Coast. And colonists liked the temperate climate of the state and insisted on moving here. Water provided transportation, food, and opportunities for business. Ports developed as early as 1726 at Brunswick Town on the Cape Fear River. Other ports flourished at Bath, Elizabeth City, Plymouth, Ocracoke, Portsmouth, Beaufort, and Wilmington.

But more light was needed. In darkness, even in daylight for that matter, the lack of any readily familiar landmarks along these low-slung barriers made travel along them a game of chance at best. In the days when ships were driven only by sail power, estimated times of arrival at ports were impossible to calculate. Moreover, ships standing offshore awaiting daylight and cooperative winds frequently encountered hurricanes or northeasters, both destructive weather systems. Enveloped by weather on all sides with no escape route, countless ships either were simply swallowed by enormous breakers or were stranded within sight of land with no help available. Many died not even knowing where in the world they were. Ships have wrecked at Cape Lookout while thinking they were at the entrance to the Cape Fear River because no landmark revealed their location on the coast.

It has been said that the state of a nation is judged by the strength of its lighthouse service. North Carolina received a lion's share of attention in her beautiful lighthouses to offer light to mariners. Between 1794 and 1966, approximately five dozen aids to navigation were built in this state. As time passed and engineering improved, lighthouses in particular grew not only in numbers but also height. Safer shipping meant saved lives and a vigorous

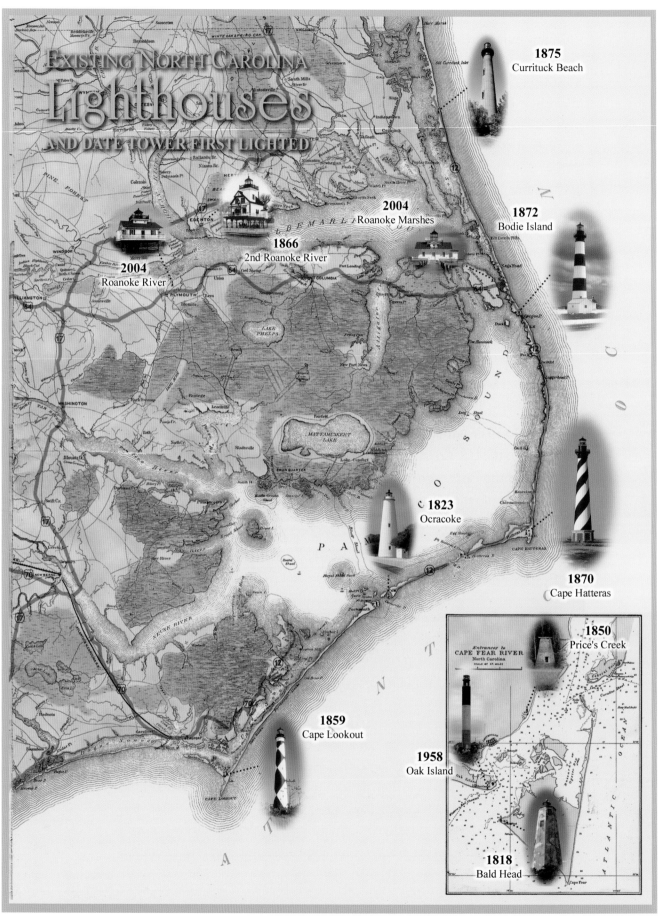

EXISTING NORTH CAROLINA
Lighthouses
AND DATE TOWER FIRST LIGHTED

1875
Currituck Beach

2004
Roanoke Marshes

1866
2nd Roanoke River

2004
Roanoke River

1872
Bodie Island

1823
Ocracoke

1870
Cape Hatteras

1859
Cape Lookout

1850
Price's Creek

1958
Oak Island

1818
Bald Head

North Carolina has nine original lighthouses guarding over 300 miles of coastline. Illustrating the continued interest in these maritime subjects, two reproductions have been built at Plymouth and Manteo. Map © 2011 Cheryl Shelton-Roberts and Bruce Roberts

economy at large. Outlasting dozens of dangerous hurricanes, northeasters, extreme cold and hot weather, and driving rain that corrodes ironwork and inundates brickwork, North Carolina's lighthouses still stand strong and shine brightly. With the help of the National Park Service (NPS) and caring, non-profit friends groups, they will stand for future generations, offering some of the best scenery anywhere in the world with salt air to season our good humor. North Carolina's lighthouses stimulate our creative minds, comfort our wounded spirits, and give us reason to publicly serve just as the lights have served us.

Author's Note

There were three distinct periods of organization in the history of the U.S. Lighthouse Service:

1789–1852 U.S. Lighthouse Establishment (USLHE)

1852–1910 Light-House Board*

1910–1939 Bureau of Lighthouses; in 1939 the service merged into the U.S. Coast Guard (USCG); in 2000 the National Historic Lighthouse Preservation Act provided a mechanism for the disposal of federally owned historic light stations to federal, state, and private, nonprofit interests.

All three names were used interchangeably, but collectively it was known as the Lighthouse Service.

*1861–1865 Confederate Light House Bureau: Following succession, Southern states formed the Confederate States of America's Light House Bureau within its own Treasury Department. Its main objective was to remove Fresnel lenses and darken the Confederate shoreline to the Union Navy. The Confederate Light House Bureau ended with the collapse of the rebel government.

This is the official seal of the U.S. Lighthouse Service.
Drawing courtesy of USCG

The U.S. Lighthouse Service hired photographer Herbert Bamber to take pictures of American light stations. He arrived in North Carolina in 1893 and took what has become rare photos, many of which are the earliest known images of these historic structures. Old Baldy originally had a brick wash. Also shown is the gentle rise of a sand dune which is characteristic of Bald Head Island. Photo courtesy of Outer Banks History Center

Old Baldy, a Surviving Soldier

In 1863, Confederate major general W. H. C. Whiting ordered the lighthouse to be destroyed so that it would not fall into Union hands. Originally, Whiting felt that he didn't have sufficient troops to occupy Bald Head Island and defend the lighthouse. However, he knew that in South Carolina, Federal troops occupied Morris Island, which helped with the successful blockade of Charleston. He then realized that Confederate occupation of Bald Head Island was mandatory in order to continue successful blockade running on the Cape Fear to Wilmington. Thus, Fort Holmes surrounded the lighthouse in 1863, and it remained in Confederate hands until Union forces took control of Fort Fisher in 1865. In all probability, this is why the lighthouse was not destroyed by either side during the war. It served as a lookout tower for what is presumed to have been Rebel signal officers, afforded a front-row seat to observe the ongoing blockade, and was relighted for brief periods during 1864 to benefit blockade runners. The distance between "Old" and "New" Inlets gave advantage to Confederates. Union naval blockaders could not effectively cover both inlets simultaneously; thus, from the lighthouse, signals to blockade runners conveyed if Old Inlet was being guarded. Cotton and other highly

Old Baldy's silhouette can be seen in the lower left part of this image. Miles of meandering marsh channels called for a guiding light into a main river's entrance. This marked the beginning of a twenty-five-mile challenging course to reach the Port of Wilmington.

An olden plaque over the lighthouse entryway documents that the historic site was established in 1817. Daniel S. Way completed the Old Baldy tower in 1818.

Old Baldy is one of eleven "federal octagonal" towers built between 1792 and 1817. It is the only one built of brick because the Lighthouse Service chose to use the most readily available construction material. It remains a private aid to navigation.

desirable luxuries were slipped out of the river to England and traded for weapons for the Confederate cause.

A letter from the Confederate superintendent of lights dated November 21, 1861, reported that the lighting apparatuses from Federal Point, Oak Island, and Cape Fear (Old Baldy) Lights had been removed, taken to the former Customs House in Wilmington, and safely stored. After Fort Holmes was completed in 1863 and Rebels occupied the island, Captain John Wilkinson, C.S.A., blockade runner, was ordered to relight the previously darkened lights. In his book, *Narrative of a Blockade Runner*, Captain Wilkinson noted his duty but offered few details. "It was deemed expedient, at this period, to reestablish the light on Smith's Island, which had been discontinued ever since the commencement of hostilities," he wrote. "At the beginning of the war, nearly all of the lights along the Southern coast had been discontinued; the apparatus being removed to places of safety. . . . Under special instructions, I was charged with the duties of relighting the approaches to the Cape Fear River, and of detailing pilots, and signal officers to the blockade-runners. . . . To provide the means of light, every blockade-runner was required to bring in a barrel of sperm oil. In addition to these aids to navigation, the signal stations were extended farther along the coast, and compulsory service was required of the pilots."

Following the war, Old Baldy was decommissioned when the second light at Federal Point took up position at the north entrance to the river in 1866. Subsequently, New Inlet closed due to shoaling, and Federal Point was deactivated in 1880. This put the old veteran, Old Baldy, back into action. The tower was painted white for several years and equipped with a fourth-order Fresnel lens as a range light paired with a ship's lantern suspended on a pole and later a buoy, to lead river traffic into a dredged river channel. At one time, according to the 1885 Light List, it became a flashing red light. Continuing its history, the lighthouse remained an active aid to navigation until it was deactivated in 1935 for the last time, although it was equipped with a radio beacon during World War II.

In 1822 a French civil engineer, Augustin Fresnel, created the eponymous revolutionary optic, the Fresnel lens. Lenses came in several different orders and were made of panels of reflecting and refracting triangular prisms. About 80 percent of any source of light at the center of the beehive-shaped lens was captured and focused into an intensive beam to guide mariners. First-order Fresnel lenses were the largest used in the continental United States and could cast a brilliant beam of light 22 miles seaward on a clear night. Massive panels containing hundreds of prisms measured nearly 8 feet tall, 6 feet wide, and weighed 1.5 tons. Cape Hatteras, Cape Lookout, Bodie Island, Currituck Beach, and the Cape Fear Lighthouses were fitted with these large lenses to serve as seacoast lights to warn ships away from dangerous areas. A fourth-order lens measured 2.5 feet high by 1¾ feet wide and reached about 15 miles to sea. These were used at Ocracoke and Bald Head Lighthouses and some sound lights including Roanoke Marshes and Hatteras Inlet as harbor and shoal lights. A

The original exterior brick can be seen beneath the cement outer-coating on Old Baldy. The covering was to protect the aging brickwork, which created its familiar mottled tones we know today. The coating caused ambient moisture to gather on inner walls and further deteriorate the brick. Restoration efforts are ongoing.

Shoaling occurs at the Cape Fear River inlet entrances and were often marked by range lights. These Oak Island Range Lights circa 1879 illustrate the typical arrangement a shorter front range and taller rear range light that were on skids to allow realignment as the channel changed. An approaching mariner lined one range over the other to identify the safe channel to follow. A keeper lived nearby for six or more similar sets of Cape Fear range lights. Photo courtesy of Outer Banks History Center

This is an up-close look at the Oak Island Range Light on the land side. A light was exhibited from inside the structure. Typically, all the river range lights held a sixth-order Fresnel lens. At Oak Island, a fog bell was sounded by machinery. For six glorious years prior to the outbreak of hostilities, vessels could navigate the river in confidence that they would not run aground on sandy shoals that nature's elements had altered. Photo courtesy of Outer Banks History Center

fifth-order lens measured 20 inches high and 15 inches wide, could reach 10 miles across water, and they were used at many sound lights to warn of shoals to vessels traveling the shallow inner sounds to mainland ports. Finally, the sixth-order Fresnel lens was called "the gem." Diminutive at only 17 inches in height and 12 inches wide, these lights sparkled brilliantly as range lights including along the Cape Fear River. However, as towers were rebuilt and refitted with new lenses over the years, Fresnel orders at any North Carolina light could vary. For instance, the Oak Island range lights in 1890–93 exhibited a fixed red light with a sixth order in front and a fourth order in rear. At the center of these lenses during pre-electricity days rested a lamp fueled by these illuminants: whale oil 1720–1864 (dates are approximate); lard oil 1864–1884; kerosene 1884–1955. In North Carolina most seacoast lights were electrified during the 1920s, first powered by banks of rechargeable batteries and later delivered by electrical power lines during the 1930s and 1940s.

> **BALD HEAD ISLAND LIGHTHOUSE**
> **Location:** Bald Head Island
> **Nearest town:** Southport
> **Built:** 1817–1818
> **Tower height:** 100 feet
> **Elevation of focal plane:** 110 feet
> **Number of steps:** 108
> **Building material:** Brick coated with cement
> **Design/paint scheme:** White mottled plaster
> **Optic:** Decorative light; private aid to navigation
> **Status:** Historic site; deactivated by Coast Guard in 1935
> **Access:** Open to public (entrance fee)
> **Owner/manager:** Old Baldy Foundation
> **For more information:**
> Old Baldy Foundation, Inc.
> P.O. Box 3007
> Bald Head Island, NC 28461
> (910) 457-7481
> www.oldbaldy.org

Today, the Bald Head Lighthouse is listed on the National Register of Historic Places. It is cared for by the Old Baldy Foundation, a nonprofit organization that extensively restored the tower in 1990 and reopened it to the public for climbing in April 1995 as a self-guided tour for a modest fee.

The Old Baldy Foundation completed a reproduction of the 1850s keeper's quarters near the tower and interprets life on Smith Island in that era. The keeper's cottage will provide a permanent home for the man-made histories of the group of islands. Old Baldy's light was officially decommissioned long ago; however, the aged lighthouse that wears the scars of time remains a symbol of the island and a significant landmark for local mariners.

EARLY CAPE FEAR LIGHTS: THE FEDERAL POINT LIGHTHOUSES

A tragic story encompasses the three Federal Point Lighthouses that stood guardian for nearly eight decades on Federal Point, now part of Fort Fisher, across the

Nothing remains of the three lights that once stood on Federal Point at Ft. Fisher, site of the Mound Battery used by Confederates during the War Between the States. The monument pictured above is located in the center of Battle Acre close to the site of the first Federal Point tower. These lights marked New Inlet that opened during a hurricane in 1761 and became a popular river entrance that allowed vessels to bypass dangerous Frying Pan Shoals. Their use ended when the inlet closed in 1880.

Cape Fear River from Old Baldy. Two were burned, one possibly victim to its own lamps' flames, and another was lost to war. New Inlet opened in 1761 after a hurricane dredged out the shallow channel, creating a new door into the river for shallow-draft vessels. It served as a shortcut for southbound traffic that no longer had to travel around the cape, risk Frying Pan Shoals, and enter the "Old Inlet." However, the flow of tides in and out of New Inlet created sandy shoals that perpetually shifted and required experienced navigators to negotiate. This called for a new lighthouse since Old Baldy was too far away to help locate this new entrance.

The Lighthouse Service paid $1,300 to Benjamin Jacobs of Wilmington to build a 40-foot-tall brick tower, cover it with wooden shingles, and paint the entirely white, a typical lighthouse design in 1816. It was an unlucky Wednesday, April

Price's Creek is the only river light still standing in its original location. It was built as one of the Cape Fear's range lights with the keeper's house behind it; both exhibited a light from sixth-order Fresnel lenses. During the War Between the States, this demure light served as a signal station for blockade runners. It sits on private commercial land today.

13, 1836, when the structure burned. During the early part of the nineteenth century, fitful lamps used crude wicks lit by unsophisticated methods. Further, the lighthouse stairs were wooden. Destructive fires in lighthouses were not uncommon, and fire-control methods simply didn't exist. Recently the ruins of this tower's foundation were excavated on Battle Acre at Fort Fisher, documented, and then covered over again.

The Second Federal Point Lighthouse

The Lighthouse Service hired Hiram Stowell in 1837 to reconstruct this light and build a small keeper's house. It was reported at this time that Old Baldy was discontinued and painted black to distinguish it from the new Federal Point Light, approximately 8 miles to the north. Federal Point Light was taken down in 1861 to give Fort Fisher's guns a free range of fire into New Inlet and deter any blockader coming too close to the fort. Its bricks became part of the fortification; its fourth-order lens would never again watch over the river. The keeper's quarters were commandeered by Confederate leader Col. William Lamb as his headquarters and redecorated in military style.

Third Federal Point Lighthouse

Since New Inlet was still heavily used by vessels bound for the Port of Wilmington, the Federal Point Lighthouse was ordered to be rebuilt. The lighthouse was begun just months following the end of the War Between the States and completed by spring 1866. The lighthouse was a 45-foot-tall, white, two-story house on iron pilings surmounted by a lantern and displayed a beam from a fourth-order Fresnel lens. The Lighthouse Service had to buy the land upon which it resided since the fort's land had been reclaimed by its antebellum landowner.

This sketch reveals a rare view of Old Baldy surrounded by Ft. Holmes that guarded Old Inlet during the War Between the States as a Confederate blockade runner passes. Blockade runners raised a Union flag to deceive Union blockaders, which seems to be the case here since no fort guns fire on the boat and blockade runners were forbidden to bear arms. Signal lights were set on the river's edge and at some range lights to signal which inlet was not guarded. Drawing from Harper's Weekly ca. 1865

Though it was a successful construction project, this little lighthouse met with great difficulty in its short life. In just three years, repairs were needed; further, these repairs went unanswered and the lighthouse's condition worsened. Finally, a man-made obstacle ended the life of this light. The U.S. Army Corps of Engineers constructed "The Rocks," which closed New Inlet by diverting waterflow from Federal Point to "Old Inset" at Old Baldy. The small lighthouse had lost its purpose; it was abandoned by

Range lights were also situated at Orton Plantation along the river. During the War Between the States, the keeper maintained the lights not even knowing for whom he worked. After the war, he was not rehired since it was determined he kept the lights for the Confederacy.

the government at the end of 1879, and in 1881, while being used by its former Keeper Taylor as a residence, it burned.

Today the site of this last Federal Point Lighthouse is marked by the presence of a magnificent aquarium, one of North Carolina's major coastal attractions.

RANGE LIGHTS DOT THE DARK CAPE FEAR RIVERSIDE

By mid-nineteenth century, there were frequently as many as ninety vessels in the port of Wilmington loading, unloading, or waiting for space at one of the docks. The wharves were lined two vessels deep and those waiting for cargo were often moored for miles downstream. No matter if there was a wait it seems, for mariners designated a tree about 2 miles south of the port as the "dram tree." As legend has it, when a sailor safely reached this point, a dram of spirits—and perhaps more—was enjoyed by all.

The Lighthouse Service implemented a clever plan to light the way from the ocean to the docks on this busy water highway by erecting a series of range lights to guide ships past some of the more dangerous shoals. With pilots steering vessels over the bar into the river and a network of range lights to mark the channel more clearly for them, it was felt that not only would commerce increase, but the trips would become safer with fewer ships stranded on shoals along two-dozen miles of river channels.

Range lights had been completed at Orton Point, Price's Creek, and Campbell's Island, also called "Big Island," by 1849. Range lights were built in pairs: The rear light was taller than the front and, from the pilot's perspective, upon lining the lights one over the other, he knew his vessel had reached a safe channel.

On the west bank of the river north of Southport, Price's Creek Range Lights guided ships through a narrow river channel. The keeper's house served as the rear range and was brick with a wood tower in the center that held a sixth-order Fresnel lens 35 feet above the ground. Keeper Hanson Kelly Ruark served here during the War Between the States. His daughter, Mary Catherine Ruark, shared a treasured story with generations of her family about standing

In 1903 the Lighthouse Service decided a tall coastal light was needed to get a light out across Frying Pan Shoals in the Atlantic Ocean. The skeleton steel tower housed a light 169-feet above the sea. Its first-order Fresnel lens would have displayed twenty-four spokes of light; the seaman would have seen three flashes per minute. This lens and the ones at Pigeon Point, California, and Cape Hatteras, would have been exactly the same. The holophotal lens (bee-hive shaped) was the invention of Thomas Stevenson in Scotland, built for him by Leonor Fresnel after brother Augustin's death July 14, 1827. Information from Fresnel lens expert and historian Thomas A. Tag. Photograph courtesy of the Outer Banks History Center

The Destruction Island first-order Fresnel lens is nearly identical to that of the Cape Fear lens. The rotation had to be in precise synchronization or its signature would "say" something else to mariners reading their Light List and they could mistake their location—and, that simply put, meant certain disaster in the vicinity of treacherous Frying Pan Shoals. The Cape Fear lens is undergoing restoration by the Old Baldy Foundation after rescuing remaining prisms from a nearby antique store. Photo courtesy Thomas A. Tag

The massive 1903 tower was manned by a principal keeper and two assistant keepers. Their oceanfront houses are now rented to the public. The tower once starkly rose above the island just behind the houses in the center of this image. The U.S. Coast Guard discontinued the light and tore it down in 1958.

at Price's Creek and watching the battle of Fort Fisher across the river when she was nine years old.

The front range light sat by the river in a 25-foot brick tower and also exhibited a light from a gleaming sixth-order Fresnel lens. The remains of this humble tower is on private-commercial property and can be seen from the Fort Fisher–Southport ferry. Price's Creek is historically significant because it served as a Confederate signal station throughout the War Between the States. For blockade runners leaving the river and rushing into nests of Union block-aders, signals from the Fort Fisher Mound Battery bearing news of blockade action at New Inlet and signals from Oak Island at Fort Caswell with news of action at Old Inlet were relayed to Price's Creek. Blockade runners could then make a choice as to which inlet to use in their escape. Additionally, it is the only river light still standing on the Cape Fear, is one of only two extant river lights, and is the only surviving, original range light in North Carolina.

Further north, near lush Orton Plantation, a matching set of lights identical to Price's Creek were built in wetlands close to the river's edge. Stories from plantation owners who fondly recalled watching the light while sitting on their big front porches have been passed through the generations.

Another set of range lights, similar to those at Price's Creek, were located on Campbell's Island about 8 miles south of Wilmington.

The last of the range lights, added in 1855, were located at the Upper Jetty on the east side of the river about 3 miles south of Wilmington. These plans were different because the front range light was located on the keeper's house and the rear range beacon was on an open framework about 800 feet in back

The Cape Fear Lighthouse was destroyed in September 1958 to avoid confusion with a new light that had been constructed across the river on Oak Island. Built of concrete with its supporting foundation sunk deep into island sands, the lantern room arrived not by a cart pulled by horses along a traditional tram of the old Lighthouse Service, but by modern transportation: helicopters. Photo courtesy of Outer Banks History Center

of the house. These important river lights were built in a time of prosperity with all intentions of their operation continuing indefinitely. But destiny would create a different fate for them.

Finally, the Lighthouse Service stationed a lightship at Horse Shoe Bend, or Horseshoe Shoal, or simply "the Horse Shoe" near Southport between New Inlet and Price's Creek that marked a shoal in the channel near the intersection of the Cape Fear River and New Inlet channels.

In the years before the War Between the States, a trip down the Cape Fear at night was illuminated by moonlight and not much more; each moonless night immersed the river in a well of darkness. An occasional whale-oil lamp might have been seen in a window at Orton Plantation or perhaps a candle in a rare cottage along the riverbank, but in the total darkness of an inky night, the beacon lights stood out like a miner's lamp in a coal mine.

LIGHTHOUSES AND THOSE WHO CARED FOR THEM BECOME VICTIMS OF WAR

With the outbreak of hostilities in 1861, the Confederate States of America created a Light House Bureau within its Treasury Department, headquartered in Richmond. The Confederate Light House Bureau made every effort to extinguish the large coastal lights and then to remove the Fresnel lenses and other equipment to safekeeping. Smaller sound and river lights such as those on the Cape Fear River were kept burning as long as possible to keep river traffic flowing with supplies to the port of Wilmington for General Lee's armies as an aid to ships traveling the river, particularly blockade runners. Some captains like Henry Swan, father of the longtime keeper of the Cape Fear Light, risked their lives to continue blockade running even after being taken prisoner and surreptitiously regaining their freedom. Though bold in their supply runs for the Confederacy, blockade runners may not have been altogether altruistic as there were fortunes to be made. However, range light keepers were steadfast in tending their beacons as long as possible—perhaps more out of loyalty to the light than to political allegiance.

Keepers were instructed to relight the lamps each night and they did as long as the supply of oil lasted. Often the keeper did not know for whom he kept the light nor did he know whether a blue or gray uniform would show up at his doorstep and take him prisoner. As the oil inevitably ran out, Confederate authorities dismantled the Fresnel lenses and hauled them to Wilmington where they were found after the war piled up in the former Customs House along with the Fresnel lenses from Bald Head and Federal Point. The keeper at Orton Point faithfully tended the light as long as possible and upon the flame's end, due to oil deprivation, the keeper stayed faithfully nearby tending a garden and fishing the river to survive.

In March 1865, two months after the fall of Fort Fisher and the river was back in Union control, Jeremy Smith, the acting lighthouse engineer and inspector for the North Carolina District, arrived off Orton Point on the Lighthouse Service Schooner *Lenox* and unloaded a steamer lens, whale oil,

This view of the Oak Island Lighthouse was taken from across the street at the Oak Island Life-Saving Station, home of famous keeper and surfman Dunbar Davis. Its light is the second brightest in the world. It is now owned by the Town of Caswell Beach and maintained by the Friends of Oak Island Lighthouse.

and some additional supplies, and rehired the keeper and told him to set up a temporary light.

Smith and his colleague, Edward Cordell, hired keepers for the other river lights and sent a letter to the Lighthouse Service asking for approval to hire assistant keepers since the climate along the river was "unhealthy," perhaps a reference to the yellow fever epidemic in Wilmington in 1864 or possibly malaria, which was endemic to the area in the 1800s. Smith also forwarded the keepers' "Oath of Office" to the Lighthouse Service, since only loyal Union men could be hired as lighthouse keepers. Official word came back to Smith that the Orton Point keeper could not be rehired since he had kept the lights for the Confederacy and no employee of the Rebel government could work again for the United States. Although the keeper had never seen a paycheck from the Confederate Light House Bureau, he had lighted the light when asked; however, it was his career's demise.

Brilliant Gems Enshrouded

All the Cape Fear range lights had been abandoned and were in dreadful disrepair; thus, the Lighthouse Service frugally decided to use post lights instead: brass lanterns mounted on poles that could burn for six or seven days before having to be refilled. Eventually, there were roughly two dozen of them on the river, increased to nearly three dozen in the 1900s, and they were tended by keepers who made rounds by boat; one lantern keeper was posted in Southport and the other in Wilmington. The War Between the States ended many things, including the bright lights that shone at dusk on the Cape Fear River.

Perhaps the best known keeper of the 1903 lighthouse was Cap'n Charlie Swan. His house could instantly become a convalescent ward where his wife, Marie, was ready to help unfortunate shipwreck victims. He manned the tower until his retirement in 1933 after twenty-nine dedicated years. Photo courtesy of Marie (Swan) Harris

Assistant keepers' families also stood by to help if shipwreck victims needed a warm bath, dry clothes, and a meal. One of Cap'n Swan's favorite assistant keepers was Captain Devaney Farrow Jennette who died in the lantern room in 1932 while they prepared for a change of watch duty. Photo courtesy of Dawn Taylor

FOR A COASTAL LIGHT, TALLER IS BETTER

At the turn of the twentieth century, a drastic change had occurred in the channel through the Cape Fear River, and a coastal light was needed. Therefore, the Lighthouse Service constructed a steel skeleton tower in 1903 at the end of Federal Road on the southeast tip of Bald Head Island. Its thirty-year keeper was Charlie Swan, "Cap'n Charlie" as he was known to islanders. It is said that Captain Charlie's eyes were as deep blue as the sea he loved. He was from generations of seafaring men and his father had also worked for the Lighthouse Service.

The Oak Island Light can be seen prominently across the Cape Fear River as a sailboat heads for Southport on a cloudy day.

A keen $70,000 was appropriated in two $35,000 increments to get this tower built because Frying Pan Shoals had become as dangerous as Diamond Shoals off Cape Hatteras. The skeleton tower, painted white, rose starkly 161 feet out of the sand. Its spider web–like bracing and eight tremendous supporting columns made it an imposing structure. The black ironwork of the lantern room housed a first-order Fresnel lens illuminated by an incandescent oil vapor lamp. Lighthouse keepers and U.S. Life-Saving surfmen worked together, and their families were especially close; they were all kind to anyone in need of help. As told by David Stick in *Bald Head: A History of Smith Island and Cape Fear*, if a wreck were spotted, keepers used signal flags to send out the alarm immediately to the Cape Fear Life-Saving Station's surfmen, pilots in Southport, and tugboat companies. All sprang into action to help a fellow journeyman.

Cap'n Charlie manned the tower until his retirement in 1933 with two other keepers, Captain James Smith and Captain Devaney Farrow Jennette, also accomplished seafarers. Jennette died in 1932 in the lantern room while changing duty watch with Cap'n Charlie, a disturbing event for the old captain since Jennette was a dear friend. His body was lowered from the lantern room along the outside to the ground.

The U.S. Coast Guard destroyed Cap'n Charlie's light by dynamite blasts in 1958. The stalwart tower resisted destruction—Cap'n Charlie was holding her up, some say—and it took several blasts of dynamite to finally bring her down. The light was then passed to a new style of lighthouse that the U.S. Coast Guard built on Oak Island on a neighboring island.

THE LIGHTS OF OAK ISLAND

The 1958 U.S. Coast Guard tower on Oak Island took over as guardian for coastal and Cape Fear River traffic following the discontinuation of the Cape Fear Light on Bald Head Island. Nineteen years after the U.S. Coast Guard assumed responsibility for America's aids to navigation, a 155-foot, commanding lighthouse was completed in Caswell Beach on Oak Island. Using twentieth century engineering knowledge, the tower was built with approximately 70 feet of foundation sunk into bedrock. The thin, tubular lighthouse is a rigid structure with merely 8-inch thick walls. The tower was created by pouring reinforced concrete into a tall, cylindrical mold, one section at a time. The lantern room is aluminum and originally held eight, high-intensity, 480-volt mercury arc bulbs, which could flash 1.4 million candlepower. When bad weather rendered visibility of the light below 19 nautical miles, its beam was increased to fourteen

A modern oil-rig-style lighthouse was built on Frying Pan Shoals in 1966 to warn ships of the danger entering the Cape Fear River. A lightship had served this rough-and-tumble duty since 1930 with the LV 115/WAL 537 as the last ship to serve watch. The light tower stands on three-foot-diameter steel legs driven 293 feet into the ocean floor. Upstaged by global positioning satellite technology, it was automated in 1979 and deactivated in 2003. It was bought at auction in 2009 with plans to turn it into a bed-and-breakfast. Photo courtesy of Outer Banks History Center

After several times of changing from one light to another in Bald Head Island's surrounding area, the old veteran still rests center stage. Old Baldy has the distinction of being the oldest standing lighthouse in North Carolina.

million candlepower, quite a spectacular sight. Its intensity has since been reduced, but it continues as an active aid to navigation shining over Frying Pan Shoals. For obvious economic reasons, the paint was mixed directly into the concrete; in fact, the primary paint scheme permeates the wall and is sharper in definition inside the tower than outside due to years of wind and sand abrasion. To ease the labor of carrying equipment up the 134 sections of ship's steps, there is a bucket lift going right up the center of the shaft large enough for tools and equipment. An electric motor under the lantern room reels up the cable. Like bookends, the ancient Old Baldy humbly stands on one side of the Cape Fear while the modern, mighty Oak Island Light sends four flashes in four seconds and six seconds of dark every ten seconds on the other.

OAK ISLAND RANGE LIGHTS

All the grand towers that have shed light upon the dark Cape Fear River for two centuries were integral parts of a network of tall and short lights as well

A dependable compass and accurate coastal charts were not available to navigators until late-nineteenth century. A lighthouse was one of the only reliable guides that a mariner was offered. The 1859 Cape Lookout Lighthouse was sorely needed in the vicinity of dangerous Lookout Shoals. Painted in 1873, the white "checkers," or diamonds, indicate east-west and the black diamonds north-south.

CHAPTER TWO

Cape Lookout: Footprints Down East

Standing on "Shell Point," a spit of land at the tip of Harkers Island, one is embraced by the waters of Core Sound. Looking southeast, the Cape Lookout Lighthouse stands in solitude across a marsh-studded sound on South Core Banks, overlooking Lookout Bight on the west and the Atlantic Ocean to the east. These waters have carried the great people who have lived here: lighthouse keepers, life-saving surfmen, boatwrights, fishermen, net makers, whalers, and all those who formed independent communities that made a living from the sea. South Core and Shackleford Banks were once a contiguous barrier island prior to a hurricane in 1933 and formed the center of local maritime activity beginning in the early sixteenth century when explorers came in search of the great western sea. Over time, the small groups of people who had resourcefully inhabited "the banks" since the early 1700s were driven away by harsh storms and changes brought by time that even self-reliant islanders had to heed. Like seeds blown upon the wind, these people took root and thrived on nearby islands. To this day, their descendants revere the Cape Lookout Lighthouse and cherish their maritime heritage.

A Veritable Treasure Island

Core Banks, named for the native Coree Indians, has long been used as a point from which to "look out" for ships, approaching enemies, fishermen returning with the day's catch, whales, and most anything for which a human looks seaward. Within sight of the cape, a lighthouse has graced this site since 1812 and is now part of Cape Lookout National Seashore. The first humble tower was damaged during the War Between the States but was not destroyed, although Confederates surely gave it a good try. Miraculously, the 1859 lighthouse also survived the war with only interior damage to the stairs.

Fortunately, visitors to the cape in the twenty-first century can still see and touch this tower and its black-and-white diamond tuxedo. This "new" tower holds historical significance since it was one of the first ten American lighthouses that defined a new genre of tall, coastal sentinels built between 1857 and 1859 by the finest engineers that the Lighthouse Service had to offer. Many of these engineers who took on lighthouse construction were West Point

1804	Congress authorizes a lighthouse at Cape Lookout.
1810	Specifications for construction and request for bids appear on the front page of the Boston Patriot.
1811	Contract awarded to Benjamin Beal Jr., Duncan Thaxter, and James Stephenson of Boston.
1812	The first Cape Lookout lighthouse is completed and lighted, a brick tower inside a wood frame with the light 104 feet above sea level. President James Madison appoints James Fulford the first keeper at a salary of $300 per year.
1845	Red and white stripes are painted on the wood frame structure to make it more visible in the daytime. Captains report difficulty seeing the light provided by the thirteen whale oil lamps with 21-inch metal reflectors.
1851	Lighthouse is in need of serious repairs as moving sand builds up against keepers' house; complaints from seafarers mount.
1852	Congress puts lighthouses under new Lighthouse Service replacing the administration of the Fifth Auditor of the Treasury.
1856	State of the art first-order Fresnel lens installed in old tower.
1857	Congress appropriates $45,000 to build a new lighthouse.
1859	New tower completed. The first-order Fresnel lens is moved into the 150-foot brick tower and lighted for the first time on November 1. Old tower is left standing as daymark.
1861	Confederates, acting on orders of the Confederate Light House Bureau, carefully remove the first-order Fresnel and take it to the state capitol in Raleigh for safekeeping.
1863	After Union forces retake the area, a smaller third-order Fresnel lens is installed.
1864	Confederate raiding party blows away part of the wood stairs in new tower, but the Fresnel lens survives and the light is put back into service.
1867	First-order Fresnel re-installed after being repaired in France. Wooden stairs are replaced with cast-iron stairs.
1870	Kerosene lamps are introduced in American lighthouses and later become the fuel for the lamp inside the Fresnel at Cape Lookout.
1873	The tower is painted with its distinctive diagonal black and white checker (diamond) pattern. New keepers' quarters are completed. The building is still standing today and serves as a small museum and exhibit area. Volunteer resident keepers live in the house seasonally.
1879	The old tower appears on the official light list as a daymark for the last time.
1907	Another keeper's quarters was completed. It was privately bought and moved a short distance in 1958.
1914	The light is changed from a fixed white to flashing—a panel revolved on the outside of the lens.
1939	The Coast Guard takes over from the civilian-staffed Lighthouse Service.
1950	The lighthouse is automated and keepers are no longer needed. Cape Lookout Coast Guard Station takes over supervising the lighthouse.
1966	Cape Lookout National Seashore established, light still owned and maintained by the U.S. Coast Guard.
1972	**(October 18)** Lighthouse station, including lighthouse, keepers' quarters, oil house, coal shed, and summer kitchen listed on National Register of Historic Places.
1975	**(September)** Fresnel lens removed and replaced with two DCB-24 aerobeacons. Its characteristic remains one white flash every 15 seconds.
1978	**(November 29)** Portsmouth Village listed on National Register of Historic Places.
1989	**(February 1)** U.S. Coast Guard Station complex at Cape Lookout, including station, galley, equipment building ("garage" with large doors), cisterns, etc. listed on National Register of Historic Places.
2000	**(June 30)** Cape Lookout Historic District listed on National Register of Historic Places: runs approximately from the lighthouse to Coast Guard Station.
2003	Cape Lookout Lighthouse ownership transferred to the National Park Service. Lighthouse appears on U.S. postage stamp as one of five in the Southeastern Lighthouses series.
2010	**(July 15)** After restoration work, the lighthouse opens for regular although limited seasonal climbing to the public.

Cape Lookout is a fine example that lighthouses are perched on the edge of safety and danger. To the left is the protection of "the Bight," a lee-side of the island that many ships sought its safety; to the right is the Atlantic Ocean and its shallow areas of Lookout Shoals.

Academy graduates who became Army Corps of Engineers and future military leaders. This tall guardian reaches an impressive 163 feet into the azure skies over Core Banks and Lookout Shoals, known as "*Promontorium Tremendum*" or "horrible headland." This ominous nametag, recorded on sixteenth-century maps, has proven well deserved since Cape Lookout marks Lookout Shoals, part of the Graveyard of the Atlantic. Lookout Shoals lurk just under the sea's surface and can reduce water depth to just a few feet in unexpected shallows. Frequently, mariners were upon the shoals before spotting land, and these wrecks, though close to landfall, were all too often fatal. Early maps, including a 1590 White-DeBry map, emphatically warned of the shoals off Cape Lookout as mariners evidently considered them even more hazardous than Diamond Shoals 70 miles to the north. But Cape Lookout also serves as a welcoming light by beckoning ships to the protective lee of Lookout Bight. The Bight is formed by a hook of sand, an extension of the cape that holds the waters of Core and Back Sounds to the west and north like a protective, cupped hand. This refuge is created by the lie of the land off Core Banks and has been valued by mariners for centuries. Historically, Lookout Bight served as a rest stop conveniently midway between major points on the map now known as Charleston and Norfolk.

Today, the Bight is a favorite place for fishing, swimming, viewing wild Shackleford horses, boating, and visiting the lighthouse. Graceful sailboats anchor for days at a time while their owners explore the area or just enjoy the simplicity of the undeveloped island surroundings.

THE FIRST CAPE LOOKOUT LIGHTHOUSE

The first Cape Lookout Lighthouse was appropriated by Congress in 1804 and, on orders of the Secretary of the Treasury, a four-acre site at the cape was deeded to the government the following year by Joseph Fulford and Elijah Pigott. A public announcement by Henry Dearborn of Boston, David Geston of New York, and Brian Hellen of Beaufort, North Carolina, was printed in the Saturday, December 22, 1810, *Boston Patriot* for contractors to bid on the specifically described lighthouse. According to the *Patriot*, its dimensions were to be: a wooden tower 93 feet tall from foundation to bottom of lantern room and its octagonal walls formed a "pyramidal" shape that were to be 3 feet thick with a 55-foot diameter sloping upwards to 14 feet and surmounted by a lantern room. The lighthouse was to be painted with three coats alternately white and brown. The interior was to contain a brick well in which the stairs ran up. The outer wooden tower and inner brick well have been described by scholars as two towers, and by all accounts, the stripes were white and red, not brown. What was actually built by Benjamin Beal Jr., Duncan Thaxter, and

This is an artist's rendering of the 1812 Cape Lookout Lighthouse. It was an octagonal tower with an exterior wood-shingled frame and a brick inner stairwell. Red-and-white-horizontal stripes made up its daymark. Its light was created by thirteen lamps with 21-inch parabolic reflectors. The focal plane of the light was 96 feet above ground level. President James Madison appointed James Fulford as the first keeper at a salary of $300 a year.
Drawing courtesy of the NPS

THE SECOND CAPE LOOKOUT LIGHTHOUSE

To date, many documents on the 1859 tower have not been located; however, existing letter index cards along with a few other documents offer tantalizing clues as to what happened during lighthouse construction.

In a letter written April 28, 1858, Captain W. H. C. Whiting of the Army Corps of Engineers based in Wilmington, referred "to the non-necessity for pilings" for the new tower. This indexed letter cannot reveal the exact nature of the foundation but can only suggest that the tower possibly rests on a pine timber grillage.

The new lighthouse was a gift to mariners that would keep on giving from the nineteenth century into the new millennia. The most modern architectural logic for the time went into its design: added height to put the beam of light out across Lookout Shoals and tall enough to rise above the morning mists and fogs; conical style to offer less resistance to wind; solid-brick construction that tapered from 8 feet at the base to 2 feet at the top for strength and insulation; and an iron lantern room that accommodated the Fresnel lens from the old tower, one of the earliest first-order Fresnel lenses to be brought into the country from France.

Improvements continued through the years including a new keepers' house in 1873, although it still was too small to house three keepers and their families. That same year, the lighthouse received its black-and-white checkered pattern, called "diamonds" by locals. The black diamonds face north-south while the white diamonds face east-west, a unique daymark for any American tower. As needed, storehouses were erected in 1889, a separate oil house was added in the 1890s for fire safety, and a second keepers' quarters was built in 1907.

The year 1852 was a benchmark for the U.S. Lighthouse Service. A Light-House Board took control of all lighthouse construction, hiring trained Topographical and Army Corps of Engineers graduating from West Point Academy. W. H. C. Whiting, top of his 1845 class became Fifth District Engineer headquartered in Wilmington, N.C., signed architectural plans for Cape Lookout Lighthouse, and oversaw its construction. Photo courtesy of Outer Banks History Center

A Lightship for Lookout Shoals

Around the end of 1904, an old lightship was stationed on Lookout Shoals to warn approaching ships of the danger. Like other lightships braving the raw conditions and tough storms along the coast, it was blown off station several times. By 1905, a proud, new $90,000 lightship, *LV 80*, took up its vigil 8 miles south-southeast from the outer end of Lookout Shoals. This placed the two-masted steel lightship approximately 18 miles from the lighthouse, anchored by a three-and-one-half-ton mushroom anchor that had proven more successful at keeping the ship on station during storms than earlier anchors. The light vessel had one white and one red mast. She certainly was a colorful addition to the area, as her hull was red from the bow to the pilot house, and from the mainmast aft, it had a bright-yellow-midship section with bold letters "Cape Lookout Shoals" on each side and #80 on each bow. For bad weather, she was equipped with a steam chime whistle or a fog bell that could be struck by hand. Since lightships were chained sentinels with no intentions of travel, it likely was comforting to the crew to at least be heard when fog made the lightship invisible. The lightship dependably stood watch until 1933 when the last of the Lookout Shoals Lightships stationed there was pulled from service.

This is an original U.S. Lighthouse Service photograph taken by Herbert "Henry" Bamber in 1893. Bamber traveled with similar equipment as Matthew Brady during the War Between the States, developing his pictures in a makeshift darkroom. The hues of blue indicate this is an original cyanotype. Original Bamber photograph from authors' private collection

Nature Rules

The year 1933 was a milestone for the Cape Lookout area as the Depression brought lean times to the entire country. Also, Mother Nature did some extreme housekeeping by brutally delivering a Category 3 hurricane to the doors of quiet fishing villages along Shackleford and Core Banks. As human presence dwindled, the area evolved into a premier example of a coastal wilderness area allowed to remain natural. On March 10, 1966, President Lyndon Johnson authorized Cape Lookout National Seashore, and it was officially established in 1976. Although the park was formed relatively late in

In November 2009, during the lighthouse's 150th anniversary celebration, the NPS announced funds were available for repairs to the tower and that it would be opened to the public for climbing. The 1859 lighthouse miraculously survived attempts by Rebels to destroy both towers in 1864; a replacement Fresnel lens was put in place and the lower stairs repaired.

comparison to other national parks, it continues as a world example of how barrier islands are dynamic ribbons of sand. The world will see an answer to a hotly debated subject: allowing barrier islands to remain natural versus permitting hardening of the coast and continuing to develop beachfronts.

The park forms a sheltered boundary for approximately 28,500 acres of undeveloped barrier islands. Touched by no bridges or paved roads, it has never been a large center of population. The seashore is comprised of Shackleford Banks, Core Banks that is broken into northern and southern barrier islands by New Drum Inlet, Portsmouth Village, and dozens of islets within the glimmering waters of Core, Back, and Pamlico Sounds. Similar to the Outer

Banks north of Ocracoke, the slender barrier islands are predominantly empty beaches punctuated by low-lying dunes and tremendous areas of salt marsh along the sounds. Native grasslands are some of the only ones remaining in the eastern United States. The dune grass anchors precious sand along the wind-blown beaches and marshland water, and marsh grasses are nurseries for shrimp, clams, crabs, and a wealth of fish and waterfowl. The national seashore does a balancing act to allow visitors to enjoy the rich history and scenery of "the Banks," as locals call the area, and yet to protect dwindling numbers of creatures and plants that make this a unique place on our planet. Amidst the natural beauty, the Cape Lookout Lighthouse is centerpiece for the park.

Wind, wave action, and tides with underwater rivers of natural currents keep the barrier islands a dynamic system that is always in flux. The islands are akin to a living creature in that over time its wounds from harsh storms slowly heal. With natural overwash, sand on the soundside waxes as a storm may cause the beachside to wane as much as 30 feet after a storm. But due to the east-west lay of the land in the bight, it is estimated that 1,000 feet of

Continued on p. 43

This is a 360 degree by 180 degree equirectangular image taken from the lantern room at Cape Lookout Lighthouse. The left side of the image begins where the right side ends. It is a composite of ten images taken by a high quality digital SLR utilizing a fisheye lens and a spherical panoramic head. The images were merged with specialized panoramic software. Photo by Dr. Laddie Crisp Jr.

Outer Banks Wild Horses

A wild horse roaming a beach is a scene that harkens back to the seventeenth century. With mane and tail flowing in the omnipresent Outer Banks wind, a wild horse is one of the remaining symbols of the famed, wild spirit of the North Carolina coast.

Four feral, or wild, herds of horses reside in protected areas along an approximately 160-mile stretch from Cape Lookout to Corova, north of Corolla. On the southern Outer Banks there are two groups of wild horses that run free on 9-mile-long Shackleford Banks. Another group is found within the Rachel Carson Natural Preserve, one of a series of islets between Beaufort's Taylor Creek and Shackleford Banks and is part of the North Carolina Coastal Reserve system. This extensive reserve system consists of selectively protected areas that extend from Currituck Banks in the north to Bald Head Woods to the south. Each ecosystem is teeming with life in the air, on the ground, and under the water, and is home to beautiful wild horses. Each group is isolated unto themselves; for instance, dun color horses with a grayish yellow coat and black mane and tail appear only in the Rachel Carson group.

These Shackleford Banks horses stand where Diamond City once existed, a whaling community that developed during the early nineteenth century and was namesake for the lighthouse's paint pattern. By the twentieth century, the community became known for mullet fishing and processing. Today, the wild horses, proven descendants of Spanish mustangs, are the only residents and are legislatively protected as one of the last wild horses in the U.S and are monitored by the NPS and Foundation for Shackleford Horses, Inc.

Ocracoke's ponies are now penned due to heavy traffic on NC Highway 12. This herd has pintos, well known for their black, brown, and white markings. Until the 1990s, the sight of wild ponies grazing on grass was a common sight along roadsides and in yards from Ocracoke to Corolla. Today there are approximately thirty wild horses on Ocracoke Island, 10 percent of the original population that once roamed these sand dunes and marshy areas, in a protective pen built and maintained by their caretaker, the National Park Service. To avoid DNA collapse in such a small herd, a new gene pool has been introduced via a Shackleford Banks stallion. New foals are expected, and the future of the herd looks promising. Over the centuries, loss of habitat and disease have taken a toll; indeed, regular checks for equine infectious anemia, which can be fatal to

Cape Lookout's barrier island, untouched by bridges or paved roads, will be a proving ground that the wellbeing of these islands will remain healthy as long as they are allowed to live as freely as the wild horses of neighboring Shackleford Banks. Photo by Cheryl Burke

the horses, are conducted. Biting flies spread the disease and force any affected horses to be quarantined. The horses of Corova lived for centuries on undeveloped beaches with little human intrusion. Almost overnight during the 1980s, commercial development drove these magnificent, adaptive animals from their homes. After nearly two-dozen horses were hit and killed by vehicles in a short time, volunteers from Corolla Wild Horse Fund moved the herd north of Corolla onto the Currituck National Wildlife Refuge. The area is called Corova and is located on the north end of Corolla Island, a few miles from the Currituck Beach Lighthouse. They now enjoy an 1,800-acre area where they are separated from humans by a 4-foot fence that extends from the ocean to the sound. Sadly, there have been incidents when humans have purposely harmed the horses. As development continues at Corova, a permanently safe haven for these magnificent wild horses is needed. Visitors may enter the refuge either as pedestrians or on four-wheel-drive vehicles over a cattle guard. The horses are like children, though, and they try to return "home." For their safety they periodically have to be relocated.

Wild horses are considered as indigenous as any other native Outer Banks resident; in fact, locals have long called them "Bankers" or "Banker ponies." Legend has it that the ponies of Ocracoke were left by shipwrecked explorers of the sixteenth or seventeenth century who often brought livestock to the New World. If a ship ran aground, animals were offloaded to lighten the ship in order to refloat it. It is assumed that the animals were then left on the islands to fend for themselves. Sir Richard Grenville's ship *Tiger* foundered near Ocracoke Island in 1565 and he may have unloaded Spanish mustangs. The horses adapted to eating tough marsh grass and digging for fresh water with their hooves in the coastal sands. As herds increased, Ocracoke had an annual Fourth of July pony penning— one of the revered memories for old timers who recall these exciting events. Just about every island boy had his own horse or could get one. In the early 1950s native Marvin Howard retired from the Army Corps of Engineers, returned to Ocracoke, and started the only mounted Boy Scout troop in America, which made nationwide news.

According to the Cape Hatteras National Seashore, Spanish horses have five lumbar vertebrae instead of the usual six, and they have seventeen ribs instead of the usual eighteen of other horses, thus proving at least some of these horses are descendants of Spanish stock. Dr. Gus Cothran, a geneticist with the University of Kentucky, who works with Cape Lookout National Seashore, performed DNA tests on the Shackleford Banks horses and has proven that at least some of the horses indeed are descendants of Spanish horse bloodlines. These horses likely had ancestors from Spain by way of Hispaniola between Cuba and Puerto Rico. Also, Dr. Cothran states they are genetically closer to horses than ponies mainly due to their larger size.

Outer Banks wild horses survive by eating tough marsh grass and digging for fresh water with hooves. Deadly hurricane Isabel swept over Cape Lookout in 2003 with Category 2 winds. At least one horse from nearby Carrot Island (Beaufort) was drowned as it tried to reach Shackleford Banks. But nature's surprise was a new foal born amidst the maelstrom. Pictured is Miss Isabel, about five-days-old, and her mother, Marilyn. Photo by Carolyn Mason

Before Grenville sailed this coastline, Christopher Columbus had brought the first Spanish steeds in 1493 on his second voyage to the New World for breeding purposes when worldwide exploration was expanding. A horse was as important to an explorer as a boat was to a fisherman. As ships passed various parts of the Outer Banks, horses were left along the islands to survive on their own. Over time, horses that were once free range and owned by island residents mingled with the herd and the breed has become varied. For instance, horses that look akin to palominos are seen along Shackleford Banks. The population of this herd is monitored by the Cape Lookout National Seashore, allowing around 110–130 horses to roam, eat, and breed.

In order to keep the Shackleford horses truly "wild," they are not treated as pets in any fashion and their diets are not supplemented by the park; the horses continue to adapt to eating sea grass, sea oats, and various grasses growing in the swales along the island, areas between dunes where grass, protected from salt spray, grows prolifically. According to Dr. Sue Stuska, Cape Lookout National Seashore horse biologist, the ponies are "picky" about what they eat. They have favorite watering holes, favorite swales upon which to eat, and areas where they enjoy resting. During summer heat, groups linger on the beach to catch the onshore winds that are cooling and keep bugs away. Each group has its own social strata with at least one "Alpha," or dominant, stallion, an "Alpha" mare,

A second herd of wild horses reside on Ocracoke Island. These horses like the ones on Shackleford Banks are monitored by the National Park Service. The Ocracoke herd dwindled to so few members that the herd was on the brink of DNA collapse. Recently, a new gene pool was introduced from the Shackleford herd. Poloma was born to Spirit in 2009 as a hopeful sign for this herd's future.
Photo courtesy of NPS

and young foals. In each of about nineteen groups of the Shackleford horses, a stallion nobly defends his "harem" of mares, which appears to be a full-time job. When a young male is old enough, certainly by three years of age, he joins one of about four "bachelor" groups, and awaits his time to become a member of another group and earn a more respected status within the hierarchy. Birth control darts are used periodically to keep the number of horses on the island at a reasonable number and to prevent overcompetition for food as well as to give a mare a break if she has foaled too often. Stuska checks the horses constantly by a "rump inspection" to ensure each of the beautiful creatures looks healthy and well fed. She never tires of watching and interpreting their communicative "body language" among group members and with other groups. If a watering hole dries up during the summer, there is competition to access one that may be favored by another group. Bachelors hang out in groups and observe the young ladies, communicating and asking permission to keep them company.

These rough-coated horses represent one of the few American wild horse species to be found today on the North American continent. On Shackleford, every few years a "roundup" is held and horses are chosen to be put up for adoption. Stories abound from those who grew up along these coastal areas and attended a roundup, selected a "pony" for their own, trained it, and rode along the beach with joyful abandon.

The "Shackleford Banks Wild Horses Protection Act" was passed in 1998 to protect the horses within Cape Lookout National Seashore and requires an annual report on the status of the herd. In April 1999, a Memorandum of Understanding was signed between the National Park Service and the Foundation for Shackleford Horses, Inc., for joint management of the horses on Shackleford Banks. For information on horse watching walks, contact Cape Lookout National Seashore, (252) 728-2250, ext. 3017, www .nps.gov/calo, or Foundation for Shackleford Horses, Inc., P.O. Box 841, Beaufort, NC 28516; www .shacklefordhorses.org.

For information about the Corolla Wild Horse Fund, visit www.corollawildhorses.com/.

Horses once roamed freely all around the Currituck Beach Lighthouse. But when N.C. 12 was paved, traffic increased; cars hit and killed several prized herd members. The Corolla Wild Horse Fund moved the herd further north to Corova in 1995, accessible only by four-wheel-drive vehicles along the beach. As people move here, the horses' domain diminishes; unfortunately, some horses have been purposely killed. Only a state-protected area like that on Shackleford Banks will solve this dilemma.

Old island natives say that the only way these barrier islands can survive is to allow natural overwash to occur. Ocean waves sweep these islands, sometimes gently, sometimes violently, toward the mainland. While one side of the barrier island erodes, the opposite side builds up; indeed the islands are dynamic as if a living creature. Hardened, one side becomes steep and the opposite side also erodes, devoid of natural sand nourishment.

The Cape Lookout Lighthouse beacon pierces the air on New Year's Eve. Early colonial officials recognized the value of North Carolina's coast. Transportation was by water, goods were shipped via water, and life could be sustained upon the bounty offered by water.

Continued from p. 36

beach between the lighthouse and sound eroded away between 1940 and 1979. Since then, erosion has waxed and waned but continues to threaten the keepers' quarters.

At one time, all the islands were heavily forested; however, trees have disappeared from virtually all the banks except for remnants of maritime forests such as Guthrie's Hammock on Shackleford Banks. A few magnificent stands of ancient live oaks and cedars huddle together in protective groups here and there. When the islands were populated, most of the trees were cut for boat making and building houses. Little did the islanders know that by cutting the trees that they were taking away the very foundation from under their feet. Other forces constantly at work, as if in a slow-motion video, are time, tide, and salt-water spray that cause the death of a forest on one side of a dune as new vegetation takes root on the protected side away from harsh elements. Like a slow-crawling creature, the sand builds up against whatever tenacious vegetation takes root near the high-tide line, grows, traps more sand, is suffocated by it, spills over to spread out and moves until it hits something else upon which to build.

Just as the Cape Lookout Lighthouse was the first of its type in North Carolina in 1859, these forever-wild ribbons of sand will demonstrate firsthand that the only way to sustain the health of barrier islands is to leave them unhardened, undeveloped, and allow them to move as wildly and freely as the Shackleford Banks horses.

CAPE LOOKOUT LIGHTHOUSE
Location: Cape Lookout National Seashore
Nearest town: Beaufort
Built: 1859
Tower height: 163 feet
Elevation of focal plane: 150 feet
Number of steps: 201
Building material: Brick
Design/paint scheme: Black and white diamond pattern
Optic: DCB-24 aerobeacon; range of visibility 19 nautical miles
Status: Active
Access: Open for climbing seasonally Thursday–Saturday on limited reservations-only basis
Owner/manager: beacon operated and maintained by the U.S. Coast Guard; lighthouse and property owned by the National Park Service
For more information:
Cape Lookout National Seashore
131 Charles Street
Harkers Island, NC 28531
(252) 728-2250; Reservations: (252) 728-0708
www.nps.gov/calo

After 150 years of service, the lighthouse received repairs including replacing the exterior entry wood stairs and landing to match those constructed in 1859, strengthening the cast-iron spiral stair treads, repairing treads that were cut to install the 1916 clockwork mechanism to turn the first-order Fresnel lens, and replacing the handrail on the gallery, including adding safety mesh to make the gallery safe for children.

The composition of this picture is quintessential Ocracoke Island: the lighthouse at twilight, classic white picket fence that leads to a small graveyard, a boardwalk to span often-wet grassy areas, and century-old, low profile live oak trees. Photograph by Mark Riddick of New Light Photography

CHAPTER THREE

Ocracoke: Treasure Island

In a picturesque Hyde County village, on a barrier island all its own, stands a harbor light. Completed in 1823, it is one of a series of lights that once welcomed vessels into Ocracoke Inlet. The first area lights appeared on nearby Beacon Island as early as 1733 as humble post-range lanterns. Next, around the turn of the nineteenth century, a lighthouse was situated on Shell Castle Island, another small island just southwest of Ocracoke Island. An additional light was established in 1853 on the keeper's house on Beacon Island, which served as a range light paired with a lightship in Ocracoke Inlet. These lights were attempts to offset the power of nature and lead mariners safely to harbor while serving the state's burgeoning mainland ports. While the other lights have faded into history, the familiar Ocracoke Lighthouse looks much as it did practically two centuries ago, still surrounded by small homes lined with white picket fences that create an idyllic, coastal village scene. Olden times are embraced in this lighthouse village that was built on fishing and shipping.

DANGEROUS ENCOUNTERS

Many who traveled this coastline had at least one close call either due to extreme weather or running aground on capricious shoals that were pushed around by prevailing winds, currents, and tides. Ship captains have often been reassured by the beam of the Ocracoke Lighthouse. But on the night of October 9, 1837, the captain of the elegant steam packet *Home* only hoped to get near enough to the lighthouse that he could find help for his passengers before his ship broke apart.

"Mr. Hunt, we little thought this would be our fate when we left New York," Captain Carleton White remarked to his chief engineer. "I hope we may all be saved."

Meanwhile, there was deafening noise as waves overwashed the *Home's* beautiful decks and angry waves ripped its hull into three pieces just 6 miles northeast of the Ocracoke Lighthouse. On deck, screaming passengers were clinging to anything they could while praying that with a bit of luck, which mariners always tried to carry with them, they could reach safety near the lighthouse.

1585	Sir Richard Grenville's flagship *Tiger* stranded in Ocracoke Inlet trying to reach Roanoke Island with Sir Walter Raleigh's colonists in June; possibly offloaded Spanish mustangs, ancestors to island ponies.
1715	The North Carolina Provincial Assembly passes "An Act for Settling and Maintaining Pilots at Roanoke and Ocracoke Inlet."
1733	Two lights that appeared on Beacon Island documented on colonial sea chart.
1803	Shell Castle Island and first Cape Hatteras Lighthouses completed.
1818	Lightning destroys Shell Castle Island tower and keepers' quarters.
1823	Ocracoke Lighthouse built.
1824	**(January 14)** Contract for fitting Ocracoke's lamps completed.
1828	Currituck Inlet closed, increasing business at Ocracoke Inlet.
1837	**(October 9)** *Home* wrecked near Ocracoke.
1846	Hurricane opens Oregon and Hatteras Inlets, diminishing business at Ocracoke.
1853	Beacon Island Light built as range with Ocracoke Inlet lightship.
1854	Ocracoke Lighthouse refitted with fourth-order Fresnel lens.
1859	**(March 3)** Congress orders a short range light at Ocracoke Lighthouse; Beacon Island and lightship discontinued.
1861	Confederates take Ocracoke's fourth-order lens, but Union restores it in 1864.
1897	Assistant keeper position established; second story added to original quarters.
1929	Another section added to keepers' quarters.
1933	Hurricane submerges Beacon Island.
1988	National Park Service, U.S. Coast Guard, and North Carolina State Historic Preservation Office preserve this National Historic Landmark.
2000	Ownership of tower transferred from the Coast Guard to National Park Service.
2010	Lighthouse restoration completed.

It is enjoyable to watch a rising sun amidst the wide expanses of Ocracoke Island's pristine beaches. But it was on these stretches of empty, featureless shores where ships ran aground trying to reach a safe harbor. The Home *wrecked in Racer's Storm in 1837 taking at least 100 souls; subsequently, legislation demanded a life preserver for each passenger.*

Flashy advertisements lured travelers by stating that the *Home* was the quickest ship sailing to Charleston. The obvious statement left out of the advertisements was that the trip's duration was dependent on weather. The ship's captain was aware of a storm in the Caribbean headed for Texas. What he didn't realize was that the storm had torn across Jamaica and Central America, entered the Gulf of Mexico, ricocheted like a bullet off the Texas coast, and was headed for the east coast of North Carolina. The *Home* encountered "Racer's Storm" near Cape Hatteras, took on water, and the panic began. Captain White decided not to beach the ship but rather to clear Wimble Shoals (near Salvo north of Hatteras) and Diamond Shoals and, if they were blessed, head for the lee of the nearest harbor at Ocracoke. But such fortune was not to be. She ran aground about 6 miles north of the island, dumping panic-weary passengers into a churning sea just 100 yards offshore. Ocracoke's beacon reached out in vain

A serene view across Silver Lake is like a scene out of a Currier and Ives painting. This light has been welcoming sailors into harbor since 1823. The light is a focal point of Ocracoke Village—like a map pin fixing the island's location on Earth.

as the doomed people pleaded for escape in a lifeboat or with a life preserver. Though the packet had been elegantly appointed and provided passengers with every convenience, there were only two life preservers aboard. Two of her three lifeboats were dashed to pieces as they were lowered over the side and the third simply dumped passengers into a violent sea that claimed approximately ninety lives that night. Ocracoke villagers helped as much as they could and opened their homes to the forty survivors. But reports of bodies that washed ashore the next day were horrendous.

As a result, an incensed Congress approved legislation requiring every ship to carry a life preserver for each passenger, a law that the U.S. Coast Guard enforces today. Moreover, the government continued to build lighthouses in an attempt to further increase the chance that sea travelers might arrive safely at their destinations.

INLETS ARE LIKE GOLD

An inlet is as good as money in the bank; better yet, it can be considered the door to the bank. British sea captains had long acknowledged that Ocracoke Inlet was a vital passage through an unsafe string of barrier islands along the Outer Banks to mainland ports. Currituck Inlet closed in 1828; thus, until 1846

when Oregon and Hatteras Inlets opened, Ocracoke Inlet was the only naviga-
ble one in that section of the Outer Banks to reach the sounds and rivers leading to business destinations including ports in Bath, New Bern, Washington,
Plymouth, Edenton, and Elizabeth City.

As Europeans began settling coastal Virginia and mainland North Carolina, Ocracoke Inlet prospered as a conduit for ship traffic to surrounding
islands including Shell Castle, Portsmouth, and Ocracoke and the mainland
ports, mentioned earlier, where some of the earliest mercantile activity began
in North Carolina.

ORIGIN OF "OCRACOKE" AS A PORT

Philip Howard, a native of the island and historian, has found over four
dozen variations of the name. He noted, "The name 'Ocracoke' is undoubtedly of early Native American origin with the first known recorded spelling

*An 1893 view of the Ocracoke Lighthouse looks little different from
today. During hurricanes the light station served as a place of refuge.
Islanders' descendants have shared stories about arriving at the
lighthouse in their boat and seeking the safety of the tower. Some even
stayed in the keeper's quarters and waited until waters receded since
this area seldom flooded.* Photo courtesy Outer Banks History Center

as 'Wococon' on John White's 1585 map."
Although the island was uninhabited at that
time, the name seems to derive from the tribe
of Woccon Indians who lived in eastern North
Carolina and who frequented the Outer
Banks seasonally to feast on fish and shellfish
that were plentiful in the area. Roger Payne, in
his book, *Place Names of the Outer Banks*, specu-
lates that Wococon could be an Anglicization
corruption of the Algonquian word "waxi-
hikami," which means "enclosed place, fort,
or stockade." To date, the earliest record of
the current spelling "Ocracoke" that Howard
can locate is documented on an 1852 map.

Though the inlet was a great help to ship
captains for reaching inland ports, it also
was a hindrance. Due to its location, water
flowing in and out carried sand and silt from
runoff originating hundreds of miles inland;
consequently, a safe inlet channel constantly
changed. Ships that drew more than 8 feet of
water risked grounding in the sounds on their
way to do business. To make an understate-
ment, this impeded development of business

Continued from p. 50

$5,000 to $10,000 savings by discontinuing the Beacon Island Lighthouse and the lightship with which it served as a range light. Instead, a mere $750 was approved by Congress on March 3, 1859, to build a short light in front of the Ocracoke Lighthouse to serve the same purpose. It appears that this was done because the Beacon Island Lighthouse and the lightship both disappeared from the Light List in 1860.

During the War Between the States, Beacon Island was garrisoned by Confederate troops at Fort Ocracoke (Fort Morgan), which was built next to the lighthouse. The fort did not last for long. Union forces chipped away at coastal North Carolina's line of defense along its barrier islands. It is reported that the fort was taken over and the lighthouse damaged in the process. The tower was still standing in 1862 but its light was darkened. Ocracoke remained an important inlet for admitting ocean-going ships, yet, the Beacon Island Light never again appeared on official Light Lists due to a significant change in the inlet channel. Without even the help of a lightship at the inlet entrance, the 1823 Ocracoke Lighthouse was left to do the job alone.

Today, Beacon Island is a natural estuarine island called a "high salt marsh" located in southeastern Pamlico Sound near Ocracoke Island. The site is protected and managed by the National Audubon Society and has long been a nesting site for Brown Pelicans, first recorded in 1928. The island is small, low in elevation and dominated by grassy vegetation. The site has a long history of use by nesting colonial waterbirds; it is posted and patrolled, and is off-limits to all visitors in the interest of wildlife conservation.

With narrow streets and sandy back roads, Ocracoke Village is made for walking, bicycling, and exploring.

Shell Castle Island Lighthouse

North Carolina's second official "lighthouse," generally defined as a tower with a light surmounted in an enclosed lantern room, was built circa 1798. The North Carolina General Assembly had begun plans for a lighthouse on Ocracoke Island around 1770 when it procured land for its erection, but didn't move forward on the idea before the federal government assumed building of lighthouses in 1789.

On the south side of Ocracoke Inlet, John Wallace and John Gray Blount, both shipping businessmen, had established a flourishing industry on a group of small islands that included a warehouse for storing cargo awaiting trans-shipment, a gristmill, and windmill. The federal government, still new to the lighthouse business, decided in May 1794 to place the light where business had already formed on Shell Castle Island, formerly known as "Old Rock Island," one of five islets near Ocracoke in Pamlico Sound. Blount and Wallace had given the humble island, made largely of oyster shells, a royal name. Land necessary for the lighthouse on Shell Castle Island was provided to the United States by the state of North Carolina and in a deed from Blount and Wallace on November 29, 1797, for a lot on which it was stipulated that "no goods should be stored, tavern kept, spirits retailed, merchandise carried on, or person reside on for the purpose of pilot or lighter vessels." Appropriation for the Shell Castle tower came July 10, 1797, at the same time a light was being built at Cape Hatteras by the same builder, Henry Dearborn. Dearborn was an accomplished man who had fought in the Revolutionary War and would go on to serve in the War of 1812; he served as Secretary of War in Thomas Jefferson's cabinet from 1801 to 1809.

The lot was small, 70 feet by 140 feet, but large enough to accommodate a wooden shingled tower 55 to 60 feet tall, a keeper's quarters, and a 200-gallon oil vault made

The Ocracoke Lighthouse was transferred to the National Park Service from the U.S. Coast Guard in 2000. A Christmas wreath is traditionally placed outside the lantern room to lend a festive spirit.

Restoration began in 2009 and concluded the next year. Strengthened steps, added bracing to the stairs, and repointing of brick (mortar) have put the lighthouse in better condition. Looking upward, this is a wide-angle view of the stairwell of Ocracoke Island Lighthouse. Photograph courtesy of Dr. Laddie Crisp Jr.

of three cedar cisterns. Completed and lighted in 1798, Ocracoke's first lighthouse is said to have been fitted with a single oil-burning "spider lamp." This was a parabola-shaped reservoir in which several burning wicks floated. It was not efficient, nor very bright.

Nevertheless, the port at Shell Castle had been important during the Revolutionary War. The British Navy was busy blockading the northern ports, so ship captains slipped past the weakly supported area through Ocracoke Inlet to the eastern shores of the Pamlico Sound and hauled ammunition overland to George Washington's troops.

A fire sparked by lightning destroyed the tower and keeper's dwelling in 1818. Following the demise of the lighthouse, Shell Castle became a quarantine area and the once-lively port became a ghost island.

A New Lighthouse for Ocracoke Inlet

By the time a replacement lighthouse for Ocracoke was approved by Congress, the main channel had shifted, and the new lighthouse site was chosen on a two-acre plot bought from Jacob Gaskill on December 5, 1822. This is the same land that had been previously owned by the North Carolina General Assembly since around 1770, but a stipulation in the contract said that a lighthouse had to be built there by 1801. Since the lighthouse had been located on Shell Castle Island instead and the federal government was just now getting around to using the site on Ocracoke Island, the plan had to start all over. Congress made a larger appropriation at $20,000, a site was chosen on Ocracoke Island, and construction began.

Considering that shipping had been shuffling in and out of the area for nearly a century at the time, the "new" 1823 Ocracoke Lighthouse was considered a youngster. Ocracoke had always been intended as a harbor light, beckoning business for mainland ports of the state. Consider that up until the 1840s, some 1,400 ships entered the inlet each year. On average, that's more than forty sets of sails each day. It must have been nothing short of a glorious sight.

Congress authorized the lighthouse on May 7, 1822, and it was built on two acres sold to the United States for $50 on December 5 of the same year. Of the initial $20,000 appropriation, Noah Porter, of Massachusetts, built the light for $11,359.35. The tower measured 65 feet tall, exhibited a beam 75 feet above sea level, and was whitewashed and topped by a black lantern.

The bright-white conical tower rests quietly at the end of a picket fence with one side of the lighthouse more steeply sloped than the other, and a lantern room that is off center. Its irregularities only add to its antiquity and character. It was built to house fifteen lamps that were fitted with oil heaters and 16-inch reflectors and revolved on a tier that was bought and installed by Winslow Lewis. Henry Dearborn executed this contract since at the time he served as collector of customs for the districts of Boston and Charleston. The exact date of lighting is not known but on January 14, 1824, Joshua Taylor, collector and superintendent of lighthouses at Ocracoke, wrote that the contract for fitting the lamps had been completed. For at least a number of years, the revolving red light made a revolution every two minutes. The fuel first used to light the lanterns behind the lens was whale oil, then kerosene, and finally electricity during the 1930s. Its electric light is now 8,000 candlepower and is visible for 14 miles.

The keeper's quarters that Porter built was a humble structure. It measured 34 by 20 feet with two rooms downstairs and a fireplace in each room. Stairs led to "chambers," which historians have interpreted as either one or three bedrooms. Attached was a "porch" 14 by 12 feet with brick walls plastered on the inside and two windows. The "porch" likely served as a kitchen area since the contract description called for a chimney with iron crane, trammels, and hooks with an oven of "middling size" on one side and a sink with a gutter to run through the brick wall. An outhouse and well were provided, giving just about all the conveniences to be had in the early years of the nineteenth century.

Ocracoke remained a lively center of trade as did the neighboring transshipment stopover at Portsmouth Island. But just as nature interrupted to alter the course of many ships, it also changed people's lives as well. A hurricane opened Oregon and Hatteras Inlets in 1846 to the north. Hatteras Inlet was deep enough that it became the preferred entry point to Pamlico Sound and mainland ports. And, as anyone could guess, business at Ocracoke fell off, reducing the torrent of business to a trickle there and on Portsmouth Island. Still supporting a light on Ocracoke, the Lighthouse Service changed out the wooden stairs for metal ones in 1850 and refitted it with a fourth-order Fresnel lens in 1854, according to the Annual Report. It then became a fixed white light. Originally, the lantern contract called for a twenty-one–pane sash set in an octagonal form, the eighth side being a door. Today the lantern room is white with ten sections of diagonal panes of windows held in place by astragals—one of the lighthouse's distinctive characteristics.

During the War Between the States the light became a prize to be won. Confederates removed

Ocracoke Lighthouse was refitted in 1854 with a fourth-order Fresnel lens, one of the first brought to the U.S. Lens orders are listed according to size and distance the light can reach. First-order lenses are largest and reach nineteen nautical miles. A smaller fourth-order lens was mainly for harbor use and reached out up to fifteen nautical miles. Photograph is taken with a special fish-eye lens and is courtesy of Dr. Laddie Crisp Jr.

Continued on p. 60

Memories of Ocracokers

Ocracoke native Belinda Farrow recalled, at age eighty-five in 2000, that when she was just a young lady, she married Clyde Farrow. He was keeper at the Ocracoke Lighthouse from 1946 until 1954. Clyde also had served on the *Diamond Shoals* lightship. He was on the *LV 105* when it was directly in the path of a hurricane on September 15, 1933. The eye of the storm passed over the lightship.

"My husband, Clyde Farrow was on the lightship with C. C. Austin the day of the hurricane [pronounced hur'-uh-kin by islanders]. He told me that when they were being dragged across Diamond Shoals after the winds shifted that the sand was rolling around in the water like it was boiling. The winds were awful and the waves were the strongest he'd ever seen. The wind and waves bent the lightship's railings all the way down to the deck. The ship was keeled over so far that he walked on the walls. Clyde came home all beat up. The President [Roosevelt] gave him a pin of accommodation and a nice letter telling him how proud he was of him. My Clyde died on Father's Day 1981."

Alona Farrow Carter, granddaughter to Keeper Farrow and longtime teaching veteran, treasures the memory of her granddaddy. "He was keeper during the time when the Coast Guard had taken over but he remained a civilian with the old Lighthouse Service," she said. "His orders to report to Ocracoke read, 'Lighthouse Keeper,' not Coast Guard. He not only had to take care of the lighthouse, but he had the buoys and channel markers to tend out in the inlet. About once a month he took batteries to go out and check the channel markers and see if the battery was still charged or give it a new one. Since he did it on a regular basis, he knew about how long they'd last. 'There's too many boaters out there and they need to be taken care of,' is what he'd say if he was told even late in the day that one was out. He had a small boat tied up at the lighthouse dock and sometimes a Coast Guardsman would go out with him and he checked the buoys between Ocracoke and Portsmouth. The buoy tenders came once or twice a year to deliver supplies and they did most of the buoy work." Alona then laughed, "Granddaddy went out on a trip and I jumped in the creek [Silver Lake] and started swimming after he left even though he had told me not to—he was so afraid I'd drown. He returned for something he forgot and caught me. I loved to swim across the creek . . . it was about as quick to swim it as walk around. As a kid, you know, you love to do things you weren't supposed to. They dredged it during World War II when a big Navy base was built near where the ferry docks are today. It was a huge installation. My great-great-great-grandfather on my mom's side of the family was

Before its historic relocation, the 1870 Cape Hatteras Lighthouse literally stood on the edge of the sea. The grandeur of its setting made for prized photography opportunities; however, the dramatic fore and backgrounds masked the tentative hold that the tower's shallow foundation created.

The crew from Life-Saving Station No. 22, Sixth District, North Carolina, also known as Creed's Hill, covered the patrol for about 6 miles around the dreaded cape. An excerpt from *Heroes of the Storm* by William D. O'Connor (1904) represents a first-hand account about these notorious shoals. "Yet his dreadful watch is made necessary by the presence offshore of a nest of shoals, range after range, which is the terror of navigators. The first, a mile wide, stretches from the point of the cape between two and three miles seaward, covered with a depth of only seven feet of water, which in storms are miles of raging foam. The formation is, in fact, a submarine prolongation of the cape. Beyond it, separated by half a mile of channel, is another formidable shoal, the Diamond, two miles long; and beyond this again, another range of shallows, the outer shoals . . ." The crew of Creed's Hill were so sure they'd never make it out and back in the broiling sea that they made wills to divide their meager belongings amongst family members before launching their modest surfboat. But this time, they did make it back with the ship's captain and three surviving crewmembers. This time, they were fortunate, but only at the whims of Diamond Shoals and with a lifesaver's luck.

Nature Laid the Course

So, one might ask, if Cape Hatteras were such a notorious area of danger with constantly shifting and changing ridges of sand at Diamond Shoals, why did mariners choose to pass by it at all?

Simply put, *they had to*. The cape defiantly elbows its way out into the Atlantic 300 miles seaward of the north coast of Florida, creating a huge obstacle. Mariners plied these waters for three basic reasons, and all of them were influenced by the Gulf Stream. First, ships traveling from the Caribbean and other southern ports utilized the natural forces of the northerly flowing Gulf Stream and southwest trade winds until they reached Cape Hatteras. The natural flow of the Gulf Stream added about 4 miles an hour to a ship's daily progress—a tremendous time saver; however, at Cape Hatteras, the stream takes a slight northwest turn before resuming a clockwise flow, passing close to Diamond Shoals, huge ridges of sand that deceptively hide just below water level. Many times ships ran upon the shoals during clear weather with no forewarning of the hazard. The fortunate ones would continue onto northern ports at Norfolk, Baltimore, Philadelphia, and New York.

Other vessels passed the cape as they were headed for Europe. Hitchhiking the Gulf Stream, akin to a river flowing within the sea, ships sailed as far north as Cape Hatteras, and then used its clockwise flow back to Europe. Early Spanish explorers returning home learned quickly that several days, even weeks, could be saved by taking advantage of the Gulf Stream.

A third reason for ocean-going vessels to venture into the cape's lair involved a southerly, one-knot flow of cold water from the north. Southbound ships had a bit of maneuvering to do to stay in the southerly flowing remnants of the Labrador Current, which pressed them dangerously close to Diamond Shoals. Mariners needed a warning signal to alert them of their navigational position and avoid the shoals. A call for a light at Cape Hatteras began as early as 1794.

In 1803, the first tower built at Cape Hatteras was a humble federal octagonal that stood ninety-five feet above the sea on a hill of sand that wind continuously depleted.
Drawing by Mike Litwin

Efforts to Aid Mariners

Efforts were needed to make shipping safer to draw business to American shores. When our fledgling nation held its all-important First Congress from 1789 to 1791, President George Washington supported Secretary of the Treasury Alexander Hamilton's efforts when he gained congressional support to enact legislation to relinquish all colonial lighthouse properties, including ongoing tower construction, to the government; today, this action is known as eminent domain. In the ninth act of the First Congress, the U.S. Lighthouse Service was born and the federal government took over the impressive responsibility to light the nation's seaboard. With the loss of lives and valuable cargoes in the Hatteras area, the Senate asked the Treasury Department in 1794 to explore building a light. Hamilton called for a "first rate light" at Cape Hatteras.

Guardian of Stone: the First Cape Hatteras Lighthouse

Following congressional debates, a specific site for the first Cape Hatteras Lighthouse was chosen. A clear deed for four acres was eventually procured in 1798 from four Jennett children, William, Jabez, Mary, and Aquilla, for which they were paid fifty dollars. Joseph Jennette, father of the children, was deceased; his wife, Christian, was listed as guardian in the 1790 census. These

Continued on p. 73

Union troops landed on North Carolina's coast and took control of the northern Outer Banks during late 1861 and captured Hatteras Inlet. The 20th Indiana Regiment bivouacked around the lighthouse, saving the tower from damage or even destruction by Confederate troops. Drawing courtesy of the Outer Banks History Center

Moving a Landmark: It Was About Time

Weighing in at a hefty 4,800 tons and stretching a striking height at nearly 200 feet tall, the Cape Hatteras Lighthouse was relocated 2,900 feet southwest between June 17 and July 9, 1999. The relocation process became a race with time to remove it from the edge of the sea. Not only was erosion threatening to claim it, but also summer hurricanes were heading for the Outer Banks.

Numerous efforts and $17 million were spent on erosion control methods from the 1930s until the 1990s. North Carolina's Outer Banks are slowly migrating westward toward the mainland through a natural process called "overwash," in which erosion occurs oceanside while accretion takes place soundside. Consequently, by 1987, the lighthouse that had been built at least 1,600 feet from the shore was only 120 feet from the ocean in spite of all available erosion control methods. Relocation was favored over further hardening of the coast with groins, jetties, or sandbags, since these methods often prove more harmful than effective.

In 1988, the National Academy of Sciences urged relocation as the best long-term protection plan and repeated this advice in 1997. Due to salt-water intrusion of the wooden foundation, wood-boring marine organisms threatened the "floating foundation," its Achilles' heel, which would have failed, assuring the tower's eventual collapse.

After a decade of debate on "move or not move," then–North Carolina senator Lauch Faircloth sought and received $11.8 million by October 1998, which gave the NPS, stewards of the light station, the go-ahead to plan and begin the relocation.

The NPS selected International Chimney Corporation, Inc. of Buffalo, New York, as the moving contractor to head a team of professionals: skilled engineers, conservation architects, and environmental scientists. Expert House Movers funded the updated unified hydraulic jacking system that was designed by Pete Friesen, a gifted structural engineer for over fifty

The Cape Hatteras relocation project began January 1999 with the relocation of the keepers' quarters and oil house 2,900 feet southwest. Move contractors dug around the foundation and dewatered so the lighthouse's foundation could be excavated.

Erosion erased over 1,000 feet of protective beach and dunes between the lighthouse and the ocean over 150 years. Groins, or steel walls running perpendicular to the beach to catch downdrift sand, caused increased erosion southwest of the lighthouse. This set up a situation that proved unstoppable; an alternative plan to save the lighthouse was needed.

As two-foot sections of granite foundation were removed, cross-braced shoring towers were installed to become the tower's temporary support. Once the total weight of the lighthouse was spread across the shoring towers, cross bracing was removed and move track I-beams were installed.

A unique hydraulic unified-jacking system was designed by engineer Pete Friesen and bought by the Matyko brothers of Expert House Movers. Groups of jacks working on hydraulic pressure supported, lifted, and lowered the lighthouse, "watched" by gauges on the unified jacking system. Sensors were installed to denote tilt. Three-zone hydraulic jack pressure allowed movers to adjust groups of jacks to keep the tower level during the move.

Hydraulic push jacks gently urged the lighthouse down the move track on the move corridor. Sections of this track was leapfrogged from behind to in front of the tower to conserve expenses. International Chimney, project manager, supervised the move from pre-planning to completion of the foundation at the new location.

years. This hydraulic system lifted, supported, and lowered the lighthouse during the move.

All parts of the light station including the brick oil house, keepers' houses, cisterns, and lighthouse were transported to positions at the new site that were identical to the original site. The move was attended by more than 20,000 visitors daily during the twenty-three days of the relocation process. The last brick was laid at 3:33 p.m. on Tuesday, September 14, 1999. The mortar had barely dried when hurricanes Dennis and Floyd rolled up the East Coast, causing damage of historic proportions to eastern North Carolina. Fortunately, damage to the lighthouse was limited to smashed windows in the tower because it was a safer distance from the brunt of severe weather. Structural engineers predict that the new setting and steel-reinforced/brick foundation will ensure the light's continued survival for the next one hundred years. The lighthouse was relighted in a ceremony on November 13, 1999, with tributes in words and music in celebration of the successful move. The tower was opened for climbing on Good Friday, April 18, 2003. A new chapter began for this cherished National Historic Monument.

Many were concerned whether the tallest brick lighthouse in the world could be safely moved. Hydraulics technology was developed in the 1950s and the center of gravity of this tower is about one-third of the distance from the ground. These two factors promised a successful relocation.

Due to hydraulic push jacks that nudged the tower down the move track, the lighthouse arrived at its destination in twenty-three days. A new era began for the Cape Hatteras Lighthouse when it settled on its steel-reinforced and brick foundation in September. It was relighted November 13, 1999.

Cape Hatteras Lighthouse
Architectural Details

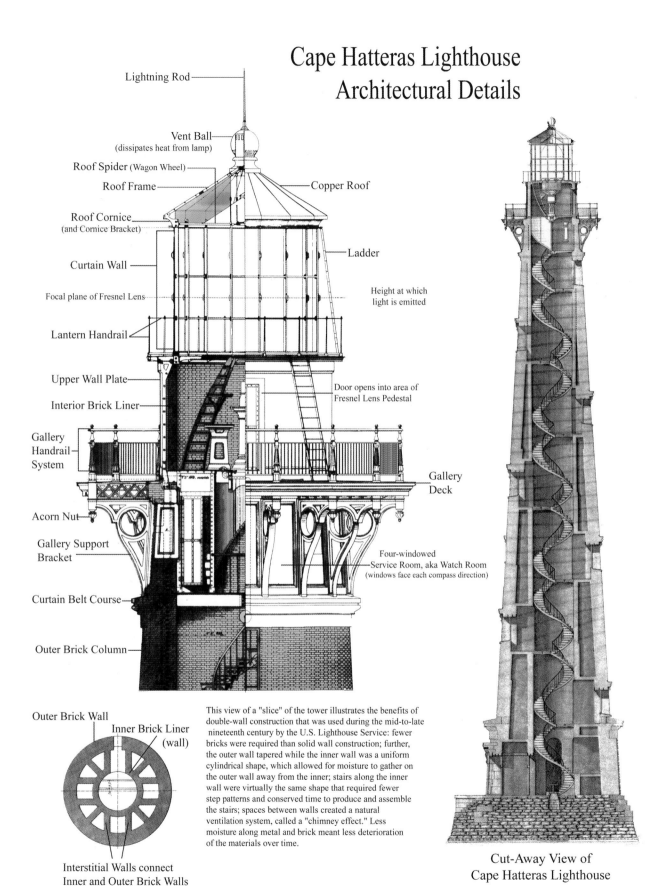

Lightning Rod

Vent Ball
(dissipates heat from lamp)

Roof Spider (Wagon Wheel)

Roof Frame

Copper Roof

Roof Cornice
(and Cornice Bracket)

Curtain Wall

Ladder

Focal plane of Fresnel Lens

Height at which
light is emitted

Lantern Handrail

Upper Wall Plate

Interior Brick Liner

Door opens into area of
Fresnel Lens Pedestal

Gallery
Handrail
System

Acorn Nut

Gallery
Deck

Gallery Support
Bracket

Four-windowed
Service Room, aka Watch Room
(windows face each compass direction)

Curtain Belt Course

Outer Brick Column

Outer Brick Wall

Inner Brick Liner
(wall)

This view of a "slice" of the tower illustrates the benefits of double-wall construction that was used during the mid-to-late nineteenth century by the U.S. Lighthouse Service: fewer bricks were required than solid wall construction; further, the outer wall tapered while the inner wall was a uniform cylindrical shape, which allowed for moisture to gather on the outer wall away from the inner; stairs along the inner wall were virtually the same shape that required fewer step patterns and conserved time to produce and assemble the stairs; spaces between walls created a natural ventilation system, called a "chimney effect." Less moisture along metal and brick meant less deterioration of the materials over time.

Interstitial Walls connect
Inner and Outer Brick Walls

Cut-Away View of
Cape Hatteras Lighthouse

Architectural drawing from original Cape Hatteras architectural plates and Graphic Design by Virginia Chadwick Howell

Continued from p. 67

four children later married and began a century-long dynasty of keepers at Cape Hatteras beginning in the mid-nineteenth century.

During the next two years, the state's General Assembly finalized the land transfer and the federal government began construction. A nationwide search ensued for a builder who was willing to brave the harsh elements and deliver needed materials. Henry Dearborn, former Revolutionary War general and well-known Massachusetts congressman for whom the Michigan city was named, expressed interest in building the lights at Cape Hatteras and Ocracoke Inlet (Shell Castle Island). Appropriations for both lighthouses totaled $38,450.

Facing multiple delays, Dearborn did not start work at Cape Hatteras until 1799. Materials had to be offloaded from boats and hand-hauled through the sand to the site, and workers suffered from a mosquito-borne illness, likely malaria. In 1802, the first Cape Hatteras Lighthouse rose 90 feet from the bare sand. Shell Castle Island Light was also completed within a year. A two-story keepers' quarters was erected at Hatteras and a vault with nine cedar cisterns completed that could hold 200 gallons of oil each. Adam Gaskins was on site as keeper; however, it would take yet another year for eighteen sperm whale oil lamps, arranged in three tiers on a revolving, iron chandelier–like platform, to be installed. Finally, in 1803, the light shone across Hatteras Island for passing mariners.

From its inception, the Cape Hatteras Lighthouse was unique among the other twenty-seven existing American lighthouses, many of which were colonial lights built with private monies before 1790, in that it was to be a coastal light meant to warn mariners to stay away from the coast, not a harbor light bringing ships nearer. As

The Hatteras Beacon Light was established in 1855 to guide local fishermen and coasting vessels that took a shortcut through Diamond Shoals via the Slue Channel to enter Pamlico Sound. Its sixth-order Fresnel lens was tended by the third assistant keeper at Cape Hatteras Lighthouse. Photo by Herbert Bamber and courtesy of Outer Banks History Center

U.S. Lighthouse Service photographer and lighthouse engineer Herbert Bamber captured the Cape Hatteras Light Station (tower and outbuildings) from the vantage point of the ruins of the 1803 lighthouse located about 200 yards southwest. Photo courtesy of Outer Banks History Center

an early Federal octagonal tower, it was built of dressed brown stone (sandstone) and brick that reached skyward 90 feet. The tower measured 26½ feet at the base. It tapered toward the top, was equipped with wooden stairs, and was surmounted by a 12-foot-tall, birdcage-type lantern. Some considered it a homely edifice, but surely it was a welcome one because at the turn of the nineteenth century there were few reliable sailing charts and few dependable ship's chronometers to determine longitude. Even compasses were unreliable due to the sensitivity of the lodestone, influenced by any iron within a ship or its environment; incredibly, a reliable design using steel needles was not available until the late nineteenth century. Imagine standing on a rolling ship's deck while getting a fix on the four Galilean moons of Jupiter with a sextant for celestial navigation. Most ship navigation was still done by "dead reckoning," a deserved term for "fatal guessing," a mariner's location at any given moment. A light in the night could be a lifesaver.

For All Its Greatness, a Dim Debut

That night in 1803, the very best light that the government could provide was exhibited. Keeper Adam Gaskins, appointed by President Thomas Jefferson, began a tradition of light that would surpass two centuries. But there were serious problems. Dominating this lighthouse's early history was eroding sand

Born in New England's shipbuilding country, Dexter Stetson was the ideal man to supervise construction of America's tallest brick lighthouse. After unsuccessfully driving pilings deep into the cape's sand, he built a foundation of cross-pine timbers and submerged them into the fresh water table to keep them strong. On top of this grillage was placed the weight of the foundation, brick tower, and cast-iron lantern room.
Photo courtesy of Auburn Public Library, Auburn, Maine

In another 1893 Bamber photograph, a glimpse of everyday life at the double keepers' quarters can be seen with at least one keeper and two families that occupied the duplex. Fencing often was built around keepers' quarters to keep animals outside the immediate home area. At this time, pigs and horses roamed the Outer Banks freely. Photo courtesy Outer Banks History Center

around the foundation due to relentless wind; furthermore, it proved to be a disappointing, dim light. The light was so faint that it could not reach out over the shipping lanes, and for years it would draw angry criticism from captains.

Sometime between 1812 and 1815, the Winslow Lewis system of lighting was installed. The Lewis system incorporated a modified Argand lamp with a parabolic reflector. Lewis put green lenses in front of the tiers of lamps, but it diminished the light rather than intensifying it, and he removed them.

"The worst light on the coast," reported one Navy captain. Another stinging review in a Philadelphia newspaper by a steam packet captain stated, "there was as usual, no light to be seen from the lighthouse." Finally, a North Carolina newspaper ran a number of complaints from merchants and captains about the light.

A steam packet's complaint led to the refitting of the lantern with eighteen Argand lamps (only sixteen were reported lighted) and new reflectors in 1835.

Within five years, Tench Coxe, collector of revenue, reported to Fifth Auditor Pleasonton that the lighting system was almost useless. Primary keeper Isaac Farrow was accused of having damaged the lamps and reflectors or having neglected his duty. It never occurred to Pleasonton that the Winslow Lewis lighting system was inferior; he just demanded that the keeper be removed. The keeper was not removed but died two years later before all the confusion was settled. With continued public outcry, a radical change was demanded. Had *Cape Hatteras* been a play, it never would have survived past opening night.

After seventy years of absence on Diamond Shoals, a lightship was again seen where extra warning was needed for passing ships. LV 71, sister to the lightship pictured above, was torpedoed by U-352 and sunk in August 1918 after warning Allied ships in the vicinity of lurking German U-boats. Fortunately, the lightship's crew survived, Although unsuccessful in WW I, the German dream of defeating her enemies right here on America's shores also survived. Drawing courtesy of *Scientific American,* March 17, 1900

War again came to the Outer Banks in 1942. Cape Hatteras came to be known as "Torpedo Junction," because German submarine captains knew that this place was the crossroads for East Coast Allied shipping. On March 26, 1942, the Dixie Arrow fell victim to U-71 in a second German effort to win a war off the Outer Banks of North Carolina. Captain Johansen dressed in full uniform and went down in a blaze with his ship. Photo courtesy of the Ocracoke Preservation Society

The Lighthouse Stands Taller

The inexpensive Argand lamps that had been installed in many early American lighthouses burned a great deal of oil, frequently became covered with smoke, and had to be constantly cleaned—a tough job within the close confines of a small lantern room while trying to handle poker-hot glass chimneys and the metal of each lamp's oil reservoir. By the late 1840s, American naval officials were demanding that the Lighthouse Service use the Fresnel lenticular apparatus that had been in use in Europe since its invention in 1822. It was only when Congress forced Pleasonton to employ the Fresnel lenses that he did so in the late 1840s. Moreover, ship captains emphasized, Cape Hatteras needed to be taller to reach out over Diamond Shoals.

In 1851, as Pleasonton's swan song, so to speak, he moved to *lower* the light at Cape Hatteras because it could not be seen in the fog. The auditor was not administering to mariners' needs and it soon would be "curtains" for him. The old tower was already suffering age and neglect; specifically, it had never been painted or whitewashed, and the foundation was being undermined due to wind-driven sand erosion.

The criticism of the Cape Hatteras Light grew to a fever pitch with reports like this one from Lieutenant David D. Porter, U.S. Navy, sent to inspect the light: "The first nine trips I made I never saw Hatteras light at all, though frequently passing in sight of the breakers; and when I did see it, I could not tell it from a steamer's light, excepting that the steamer's lights are much brighter . . . it is still a wretched light." The Lighthouse Service took serious note and things began changing rapidly.

In 1852, Pleasonton was relieved of his lighthouse duties and the service was reorganized. In 1853, Congress authorized $15,000 in March to heighten the tower to 150 feet, install a first-order Fresnel lens, and erect a new keepers' house to replace the old one. By 1854, the lighthouse had a new look with its taller stature whitewashed for the first 70 feet and the remainder was painted red to serve as a daymark. Due to extensive improvements, at last, America's

The dual aerobeacon provided light when the lighthouse was relighted in 1950 after it became part of Cape Hatteras National Seashore. The site of the 1803 tower's ruins are seen at ground level where the boardwalk meets a sandy road that leads off to the right.

A lightship had stood watch over Diamond Shoals continuously between 1897–1967, but rough sea conditions encouraged the U.S. Coast Guard to build a modern Texas-oil-rig-style lighthouse complete with helipad. The WLV 189 *moves into lightship history. Technology marched on and absorbed the Texas tower in only a decade by 1977. Technology progressed with Global Satellite Positioning and outdated the tower; it was deactivated in 2001.* Photo courtesy of Outer Banks History Center

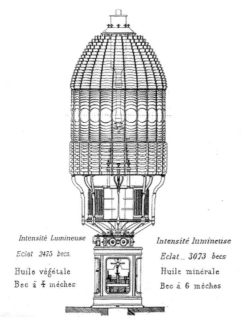

Intensité Lumineuse
Eclat 2475 becs.
Huile végétale
Bec à 4 mèches

Intensité lumineuse
Eclat.. 3073 becs
Huile minérale
Bec à 6 mèches

This drawing illustrates a first-order Fresnel lens with twenty-four bulls-eye panels to intensify light from a source at its center. At ⅓ revolution per minute, a mariner would see one flash lasting 1.5 seconds followed by a six-second eclipse (dark), creating eight flashes per minute. A lamp's flame sat in the middle with a chimney leading out the top of the lens. A Fresnel lens lost only 20% of its light whereas old lighting systems lost over half. The remains of the Cape Hatteras lens is on exhibit at the Graveyard of the Atlantic Museum on Hatteras Island.

first-rate lighthouse was able to do a better job in warning ships of Diamond Shoals.

Outbreak of Hostilities

In 1860, with war clouds rolling across the Outer Banks, Cape Hatteras was recognized as the most needed light along the coast. After the firing on Fort Sumter, North Carolina governor John W. Ellis followed South Carolina's lead and ordered all coastal lights darkened, taking away any advantage that the lighthouses may have given Union naval and land forces. Going a step further, the Confederate government in Richmond set up their own Light House Bureau and quickly realized that the lights along the Southern coast were of greater help to the Union Navy and ordered their soldiers to remove Fresnel lenses from major coastal lights and take them inland for safe storage until the war ended. Confederates removed the prized first-order Fresnel lens under the supervision of Cape Hatteras keeper Benjamin Fulcher, carefully packed the crown glass prisms and twelve bulls-eye panels in cotton within forty-four boxes, and sequestered the apparatus from Union forces in a town north of Raleigh.

The lighthouse was threatened with destruction by Rebels when Union forces were moving northward from Forts Hatteras and Clark to take control of the Outer Banks. National Park Service historian F. Ross Holland wrote: "But the Confederates had other ideas. The 3rd Georgia Infantry assaulted and routed the Federal troops in what became known as the Chicamacomico Races, and the commander, Colonel A. R. Wright, vowed, 'We will demolish the light at Hatteras if we do no more.' After retreating down the banks, the Federals stopped at Cape Hatteras, many of them sleeping on the ground around the lighthouse tower. Here they were reinforced, mustered their courage, and counterattacked the Rebels; thus the lighthouse was saved from the same fate that befell neighboring Bodie Island light tower."

Continued on p. 84

Keepers' Families Recollections

Keeper Unaka Jennette was the longest-serving keeper at Cape Hatteras (1919–1939). His son, Rany, was an industrious lad and expected to help with chores, including climbing the tower each day to polish brass. He loved to watch his father feed kerosene from the five-gallon brass can that had been carried up the 268 steps each day to the mantle lamp, trim its wick, clean the slender, graceful chimney glass, and then begin the daily cleaning of the hundreds of prisms of the first-order Fresnel lens; the lamp at the center of the lens was lit one-half hour before sunset. Rany strived to be the perfect keeper's son, but sometimes boredom at the light station lured him into mischief.

Myrtle and Rany Jennette, children of Principal Keeper Unaka Jennette and "Miss Sudie," were so close in age that they were considered twins. Both were expected to help at the light station with various chores. They loved storms, too, and the treasures to be found following a storm including timbers, buttons, coins, driftwood, and intricately patterned seashells. Photo courtesy of Rany Jennette

National Geographic photographer Clifton Adams captured Keeper Jennette, known by locals as "Capt'n 'Naka," cleaning the first-order Fresnel lens a short time before two hurricanes caused great damage to the light station. Although the keepers' houses were electrified in 1934, family life at the station ended. The lighthouse closed and a light was established in a steel tower in nearby Buxton Woods after Keeper Jennette darkened the Hatteras Lighthouse May 12, 1936. A dual aerobeacon provided a light with the same flash characteristic as the 1870 tower. Photo courtesy of NPS

A vat of tar sat beside the granite steps leading to the entrance of the lighthouse, and being summer, it was quite thin—the consistency of paint. A paintbrush or two was no problem to locate. Rany and a friend decided that the base of the tower needed a little sprucing-up. When Keeper Jennette saw the tar-stained base, he demanded to know who was responsible for the deed. Rany proudly accepted credit. Keeper Jennette was obviously angry about his son's well-intentioned deed. But Rany would have a three-day wait before finding out what his father was going to do about the situation because his father had to pick up district inspector "Captain" King in Norfolk, a long trip back then. After the inspection, Rany's father approached him with a leather razor strap and Rany knew his father did not intend to shave—his face, that is.

Rany loved to swim in the ocean, hunt for things that washed up after a storm, and to ride Wildfire, his favorite pony. Wildfire was one of the wild horses that once grazed and roamed freely on the island. "We didn't miss electricity or plumbing," Rany said frankly. "As long as the Hatteras Light worked, that's what mattered. It flashed one-and-a-half seconds on and six-seconds eclipse. I saw that flash every night through my bedroom window. It put me to sleep."

Rany's sister, Myrtle, remembered: "All I can say is that we had a wonderful life. Some thought we were so isolated from the rest of the islanders, but we didn't know any different then. We had all the Casey and Quidley children to play with, and we had lots of toys. I remember going up the stairs to the top of the lighthouse many, *many* times. I can remember clearly seeing my dad draw back the

1837	Lt. Napoleon Coste, commander of Revenue Cutter *Campbell*, explores coast south of Chesapeake; Coste calls for new light on or near Bodie Island or Pea Island.
1838	Congress asks for light in same area as Coste.
1846	Hurricane opens Oregon Inlet.
1847	First Bodie Island Lighthouse authorized by Act of Congress March 3rd; exact lighting date unknown but thought to be spring 1848.
1852	Congress reorganizes U.S. Lighthouse Service and employs Topographical and Army Corps of Engineers to design, locate, build lighthouses.
1854	U.S. Lighthouse Service installs fourth-order Fresnel lens; tower at least 1 foot out of plumb, revolving lens malfunctions.
1858	Congress appropriates $25,000 for new tower completed in 1859 with third-order lens.
1861	Retreating Confederates remove prized Fresnel lens and later destroy tower.
1871	**(June 13)** Fifteen acres purchased from John B. Etheridge and wife for $150 to replace destroyed lighthouse 1½ miles north; work begins in November.
1872	**(October 1)** New lighthouse exhibits fixed white light; duplex keepers' house completed; **(October 19)** Wire screen installed to protect lantern glass after geese crash into it.
1873	Lighthouse painted with black and white horizontal bands.
1874	Third assistant keeper's job eliminated, held by Rebecca Hatsel, only female keeper ever documented to serve at Bodie Island Light Station.
1877	Lightning strikes new tower causing minor vertical cracks; keeper on stairs feels big strike that numbs lower half of his body.
1878	The Bodie Island Life-Saving Station built 1 mile north of lighthouse; Pea Island Life-Saving Station (historic, all-black crew) completed on south end of Pea Island.
1912	Incandescent oil vapor lamp installed; increased candlepower over five times.
1922	Second assistant keeper position eliminated; increased salaries of remaining keepers.
1932	Generator that charged banks of batteries installed; powers the flash controller that turned electric light bulb off and on to present-day flash characteristic.
1939	In economic attempt to protect American shores amidst concerns about German submarines, FDR asks U.S. Coast Guard to assume lighthouse responsibilities.
1940	Keeper Vernon Gaskill Sr. transferred to Coinjock Lighthouse Depot; keeper Julian Austin Sr. stays, then retires; lighthouse automated.
1942	German U-boats attack Allied shipping off the Outer Banks.
2000	**(July 13)** Lighthouse transferred from Coast Guard to National Park Service.
2005	**(April 25)** USCG transfers Fresnel lens and lamp operation to NPS.
2006–2011	Studies and restoration funding completed; first-order Fresnel lens removed and stored; ironwork and interior brickwork begins.

Beyond the Bonner Bridge that spans Oregon Inlet to join Hatteras and Bodie Islands are the sites of the first two Bodie Island Lighthouses that are now underwater. The inlet migrates south, two miles since it opened in 1846, while swallowing everything in its path on its south side.

pointed out that guiding a sailing ship is not like steering a car. Changing of sails and gaining the right wind from the right direction takes time for making adjustments to get a ship that is running close to shore directed further out to sea. On the other hand, northbound ships for Norfolk and Baltimore needed a light after Cape Hatteras to safely keep a bearing well off the coast.

Collector of customs Thomas H. Blount was assigned the task to purchase land for the site at that time; however, it proved more easily said than done to find land with a clear deed on a sparsely populated island during the mid-nineteenth century. After five years and no deed had been procured, worries aplenty existed due to the number of ships and amount of cargo being lost in the vicinity of Bodie Island as witnessed in Blount's letter to a congressman.

"I presume the reason why it [lighthouse] has not been commenced is that the appropriation was insufficient and will require one of the first class

A modified Argand Light was used in early American lighting systems. Silver parabolic reflectors brightened the light from a wick inside the slender chimney. Fourteen of these whale-oil burning lamps were hung in chandelier-style tiers for the Bodie Island Lighthouse, first lighted in 1848. Drawing of tiers of whale-oil lamps from *London Illustrated Times* Jan. 5, 1884, courtesy of Thomas A. Tag

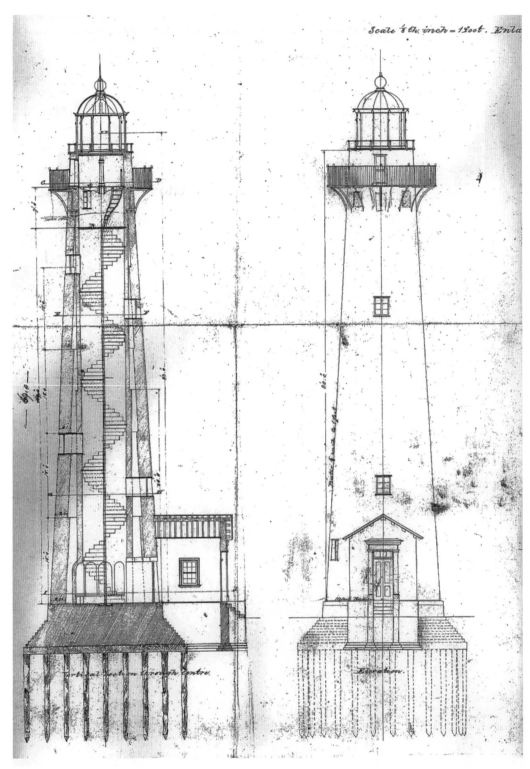

Scale ⅛th inch = 1 foot. Enla

The 1859 Bodie Island Lighthouse was a new design using the best materials available. This drawing was signed by topographical engineer Lorenzo Sitgreaves. The tower fell victim to the War Between the States when it was only two years old. Original drawing courtesy of the Outer Banks Lighthouse Society

Heeding two previously learned lessons about erosion in Oregon Inlet, the U.S. Lighthouse Service built the 1872 tower well to the north. Herbert Bamber photographed the light station in 1893. Photo courtesy of Outer Banks History Center

[lights]. There is no part of the Coast of the U.S. which requires a Light House more than Body's Island–'tis in the direct route of all going North or South & of all foreign vessel bound into the Chesapeake, & when there during the last summer, there were fifteen wrecks in sight at one place, & within the last month, a Brig bound into Norfolk was wrecked there worth more than would have built the light house."

Delayed by deed problems and procuring materials to be delivered to the site, nearly ten years passed before the first light at Bodie Island was completed in September 1847. Builder Francis A. Gibbons erected the 57-foot tower that housed fourteen Argand lamps, which were fueled by whale oil and 21-inch silver reflectors. However, trouble lay ahead.

During a three-decade stretch that lasted until 1852, all business of the Lighthouse Service remained under the auspices of the Fifth Auditor of the U.S. Treasury, Stephen Pleasonton, who made his historic distinction when he rescued the Declaration of Independence and other valuable documents from burning during an 1814 British raid on Washington, D.C. But, he was a frugal bureaucrat and he frequently sacrificed quality and beauty in lighthouse construction in the name of economy. Without a solid foundation—not the fault of Gibbons who went on to build fine West Coast towers—the lighthouse leaned until the revolving chandelier of lamps was thrown out of sync and rendered useless; moreover, erosion took what tentative footing the tower managed. This original site is now underwater at the east entrance to Oregon Inlet.

Upon the loss of the first Bodie Island Lighthouse in 1858, over 100 miles of undistinguished coast between Cape Henry and Cape Hatteras lay in total darkness. Mariners plying these waters were at the mercy of a compass and charts that were woefully inaccurate due to the dynamic nature of the ever-changing shoals along the Outer Banks.

Bodie Island served to warn southbound ships to turn eastward away from shore. In June, 1921, the wooden schooner Laura A. Barnes *was caught too near shore in a northeaster storm and waves pounded her to pieces.*

A New Era for Lighthouses and a Second, Short-Lived Light for Bodie Island

In response to mariners' complaints that a light was critical at Bodie Island, the newly organized Lighthouse Service kept its promise to build only the finest structures in its quest to make the American Lighthouse Service the best in the world. In 1859, a 90-foot white tower was completed from quality materials and housed a third-order Fresnel lens. Design and construction was under supervision of topographical engineer Lorenzo Sitgreaves. Unfortunately, tragedy occurred shortly after the start of hostilities between the North and the South and this second lighthouse was struck down before its time like a young War Between the States soldier. After Union troops had landed and taken control of the Outer Banks in 1861 during the Burnside Campaign, retreating Confederates, who had earlier removed the prized Fresnel lens, then destroyed the lighthouse, thus depriving the Union of a light to aid its naval patrols or a lookout tower from which to watch military action on Roanoke Island. Again, this stretch of perilous coast became embraced by darkness each night.

The golden era of lighthouse construction had begun before the war during the 1850s, introducing double-wall construction that allowed a lofty height of at least 150 feet to house a first-order Fresnel lens; indeed, these tall coastal lights were also called Lighthouses of the First Order. The beautiful lenses from Paris, France, were prized devices that intensified and focused a light at least 19 nautical miles seaward. The War Between the States had halted new lighthouse construction with incomplete plans left on architects' drawing boards in April 1861. Following the war, Congress helped the healing process of a battle-worn country by getting back to the business of repairing and rebuilding lighthouses to boost the nation's unsteady maritime economy.

Third Time's a Charm

The third Bodie Island Lighthouse, completed in 1872, is a prime example of the classic "tall coastal lighthouse" that utilized a timber and granite foundation, dressed granite accents, marble floors, brick walls, and ornate ironwork, nearly identical to that at Cape Hatteras. It remains one of the few lights in America with its original first-order Fresnel lens. Restoration efforts, both interior and exterior, began during 2009 and are still ongoing. When completed, its lambent, amber light again will greet us when crossing the Bonner Bridge from Hatteras Island. Its soaring beauty will again dominate the sandy and water-studded landscape.

Continued on p. 100

Memories from Keepers' Families

By the turn of the twentieth century, only two keepers were on duty, but it still made for crowded conditions when both keepers and families were in residence. We can gain some insight into what life was like there through interviews with keepers' children, now in their eighties and nineties. John Gaskill, son of keeper Vernon Gaskill Sr. remembered, "We shared the quarters with no arguments. As much as possible, one keeper and his family stood duty while the other family returned home for a while. And when we were at the lighthouse, we could use the other side of the house for visiting family or whatever. We got along just fine."

"When I think of Bodie Island, I think of home and a safe feeling," reminisced Marilyn Austin Meads, daughter of keeper Julian Austin Sr. "I had to learn to cook from the time I could reach the iron stove because Momma was in the hospital for years. I remember Daddy carrying a big bucket of coal for the warming stove and a five-gallon brass can of kerosene up those stairs with him nearly every night he was on duty. I was happy as long as I was with him." Marilyn's older brother, Julian Jr., had to keep the wood box next to the cook stove well stocked and make sure little sister was cared for while their father tended one of the most important lights on the East Coast. While mother Katherine Austin was hospitalized, Grandma Dobbs took care of the youngest, Verna. It was a happy day when their mother and Verna returned to be with the family at the lighthouse permanently in 1937. "To celebrate the occasion, Mr. Gaskill provided us with a pheasant for our Christmas dinner," Marilyn said softly. "Julian and I still talk and laugh about things we did together as kids. We loved to go down to the beach and watch the fishermen haul in their long nets. Daddy helped out some and they gave him all the fish he wanted. The fishermen had one-room sheds where they kept a coffee pot and a bed. Daddy took the fish back to the lighthouse where he had a table for cleaning them. Sometimes he put them in a big wooden barrel with salt. When we wanted to eat some, we'd soak the fish and then fry them. But I didn't like oysters when I was young. Seemed like the more I chewed the bigger they got!"

Keeper Gaskill's son, John, climbed the tower each day to extinguish the lamp and pull the canvas curtains for his keeper-father, especially during summers when he lived there full time. In later life, he volunteered at the lighthouse sharing memories with visitors about growing up at this lighthouse.

Keeper Julian Austin Sr. served at Bodie Island during the 1930s, leaving only after complete takeover by the U.S. Coast Guard in 1940. His children pictured above, Marilyn and Julian Jr., remembered the island as "home." Photo courtesy of Marilyn (Austin) Meads

The incandescent oil vapor lamp like the one above, installed at the center of the first-order Fresnel lens in 1912 vastly increased the light's intensity. During the 1920s and '30s, both keepers' sons helped to prepare and extinguish this lamp as part of their light station chores.

A keeper's family ran a marathon to keep up with maintenance at the lighthouse. Every bit of rust, tarnish, peeled paint, and broken parts of the light station were promptly repaired or replaced. The work was shared by all and children were expected to work hard. John and Julian Jr. both stated that their fathers expected them to keep the grass cut around the tower and the keepers' quarters. John said, "It was one of those push mowers and that was a *lot* of grass out there!"

Both boys helped with the incandescent oil vapor lamp by extinguishing it just after sunrise and drawing the curtains to protect the Fresnel lens from the harsh sunlight. "I remember when the light didn't flash—it was what you call 'fixed.' The Lighthouse Service installed heavy mesh wire around the light to keep geese from flying into the light. But despite this effort, some would get

Visitors were to be greeted cordially at every American light station. Tours were given to those making the effort to reach this remote station by driving the beach at high tide. Young Marilyn Austin, pictured front and center, loved to take tourists to the top and earn a small tip, enough for a rare movie and a candy treat in Manteo. Photo courtesy of Verna (Austin) Wall

killed anyway. They would fly into the lantern room and break the storm panes. And, yes, sometimes we'd have goose for dinner the next day," Julian Austin chuckled.

Playtime for the lighthouse kids included hunting for turtle eggs, rowing a small skiff into the pond near the lighthouse, and hunting for treasure on the beach following a storm. "We loved 'hurrikins' because we would lean into the wind and let it hold us up," Gaskill said with a smile.

And, just as all kids get into a bit of roughhousing, lighthouse kids had mishaps as well. John laughed as he recalled: "We used to start at the top of the stairs and run down them like a race. We'd slide down the rail a few feet, then jump several steps, over and over. One day my brother, Vernon Jr., fell and bit his tongue. There was a piece about the size of your little fingertip hanging off. He ran to the lantern room where Daddy was finishing trimming the wick and getting the lamp ready for work that night. He looked at Vernon's tongue, took his wick trimming scissors and snip! That solved the problem. I guess that's what you call lighthouse first aid!"

The Austin children had other medical emergencies. When Verna was just a wee lassie, she was sitting on the back of another child's bike. He forgot the young girl was sitting on the back and swung his leg over the bike to get off and knocked her to the brick walkway. Keeper Austin was soon in his Model T taking his little daughter to the doctor. Verna grimaced, "I remember the ride all the way to the doctor in Manteo because my arm jiggled all the way! I remember the doctor strapped it to my body and all I could do was wiggle my little finger. It was terrible."

Living at Bodie Island even in the 1920s and '30s was a pioneer's way of life. This was still a time when water was the only way to travel among the islands. An automobile was not present until the late 1920s and a bridge finally linked Bodie Island to Roanoke Island in 1928, when the Austin and Gaskill children could attend school in Manteo. Until that time, the beach side of the island was occupied only by a few fishing shanties and the Bodie Island Life-Saving Station. There were cisterns for storing rain water, the only source of fresh water. Families used an outside hand pump as well as one at the kitchen sink from which to draw water for cooking, baths, and washing dishes or clothes. Outside "privies" were used as bathrooms but the hope to get indoor bathrooms never diminished. Keeper Gaskill finally got his wish when the Lighthouse Service installed a bathtub and plumbing to pump water to his bathroom during the 1930s. Keeper Austin's children remember the day he prepared to lounge in his beloved bath when they heard a yelp coming from Gaskill's upstairs bathroom. Apparently the chilly water dampened the promise of soothing baths since there was no way to get hot water into the house. From then on, Gaskill's daughter, Erline, used the space as a playroom while on the other side of the house, Austin's son, Julian Jr., slept peacefully in their "bathroom" for several years.

Keepers kept busy with chores and when spare time was on hand, they read a great deal. Both keepers Austin and Gaskill were respected as well-read people with a great knowledge of history. Like hundreds of keepers all around America, they took advantage of the traveling library that arrived with about three dozen titles including *National Geographic* magazine and the classics. In 1876 portable libraries had been offered by the Lighthouse Service to keepers at remote light stations and all light vessels. Each library was a handsome wooden tri-fold cabinet about 2 feet high by 3 feet wide with a heavy brass handle and hardware to endure rough handling aboard lighthouse tenders. Tenders visited each light station to deliver maintenance supplies as well as these libraries. Each cabinet was numbered and contained a printed listing of the contents posted inside the door. At least every six months, these libraries were picked up and exchanged for a new one. Materials within were carefully screened for appropriateness and changed out as some publications became outdated. Keepers, wives, and children alike poured over these printed treasures because an occasional radio, Victrola, or piano were their only alternate sources of entertainment.

Continued from p. 95

Expert workmanship is built deep into this enduring lighthouse. Some of the key people involved in its design and construction were: Major George Elliot, Engineering Secretary and architect; Capt. Peter C. Hains, Fifth District lighthouse engineer and director during erection; and Dexter Stetson, superintendent of construction who had recently successfully completed Cape Hatteras Lighthouse. During the late 1830s West Point graduates in the top of their classes became members of the elite Army Corps of Engineers and Topographical Engineers. American lighthouse construction was directly influenced by emerging science and these brilliant students of engineering. Lighthouses prominently represented societal changes and the Lighthouse Service continued to stay on the cutting edge of technology.

Visitors often question the location of the Bodie Island Lighthouse as it appears to be set far back from the ocean. Some even think that it has been moved! But in reality, the first two sites were adjacent to one another near Oregon Inlet. Both are underwater, swallowed by the southerly migration of the inlet. The Lighthouse Service had learned a harsh lesson and the third tower was erected on a site away from the eroding inlet, nestled halfway between ocean and sound and serving mariners on all surrounding bodies of water.

As we look at the lighthouse today, its quiet beauty belies the tremendous efforts that were expended in its creation. Just getting the materials to

The original name of this light station is revealed in a marble plaque as "Body's Island."
Each lighthouse received a similar plaque stating the station's name, the date the site was
established, and its latitude and longitude. Likely a government clerk's error changed the
name's spelling. Within an official document three or more spelling variations can be found.

the remote site was a struggle. Stetson had broken down the workhouses at Cape Hatteras in June 1871 and moved them and leftover brick to an area that became known as "Stetson's Channel" on the sound side of the island near the lighthouse. New construction materials had to be delivered by way of Roanoke Sound because no landing access was to be had on the oceanside of the site, too rough a route to chance loss of materials. A good portion of the deliveries were made by the Lighthouse Service tender *Tulip*. Initially, the Service wanted all cut stone for the foundation; however, after weeks of delay, it reluctantly accepted partial fill for the foundation in the form of rubble stone. Further, delivery of foundation stones was delayed for three months because heavily laden schooners, sailing out of Baltimore, could not negotiate the shallows of the sound. Stetson was ordered to build a 12-foot by 12-foot pier/wharf for offloading construction materials, also built from recycled materials after finishing Cape Hatteras. McClenahan & Brothers held a contract for the foundation granite and provided a derrick. Nicholas M. Smith and Andrews &

Art imitates nature in the lighthouse's nautilus-like stairs. Keepers climbed at least twice each day to tend the lamp. Photo courtesy of Kim Fahlen of Lighthouse Lamp Shop

"Stick style" architecture is also known as Carpenter Gothic of the early 1800s and revived as Renaissance Gothic in the late 1800s with fine wood embellishments including finials at the gable ends. The style became a signature of N.C. lighthouses and Outer Banks architecture.

Rainbow spectrums are cast by prisms of Bodie Island's first-order Fresnel lens across the entry door to the lantern room. During the 1920s, a "call bell" was installed near the flame of the lamp. If something went wrong, the bell sounded in the keepers' quarters and recorded the incident on a sheet similar to graph paper. Though the bell was a convenient warning system for the keeper, it did not look good on his record if the bell had to sound.

The first-order Fresnel lens is a magnificent bee-hive-shaped masterpiece of crown glass by Barbier & Fenestre of Paris, France. Photo is an HDR "pano" (panoramic), a composite created by merging five fisheye images. This perspective captures the lantern room suspended 160 feet above marshland and ponds between the Atlantic Ocean and Roanoke Sound. Photo by Dr. Laddie Crisp Jr.

neteenth century workmanship meets twenty-first century technology in this fisheye-lens view of the Fresnel lens's canopy. Photo by Dr. Laddie Crisp Jr.

A rare Outer Banks snowfall transforms the Bodie Island Light Station into a wintry scene.

e of this light station's greatest attributes is its lack of twenty-first tury intrusions because it is protected within an undeveloped a of Cape Hatteras National Seashore.

This moonrise at the Bodie Island Lighthouse could have been nearly 150 years ago or just yesterday.

Johnson of Baltimore held contracts for brick and dressed granite, respectively. Paulding, Kemble & Co. of West Point Foundry, New York, supplied ironwork. A volunteer, Jack McCombs, recently discovered that iron beams, which secure the iron landings to the brick tower, were produced by Phoenix Iron Co. in Philadelphia and shipped to Baltimore for which the Lighthouse Service paid cash. To move this voluminous amount of materials, a small railway, called a "tram," was built, horses pulled the cars, and laborers finished the job by hauling materials to the building site. Stetson was further delayed because there was constant threat of mosquito-borne illnesses that dogged the building crew.

In *A History of the Bodie Island Light Station* (1967), National Park Service historian F. Ross Holland detailed how Stetson built the underpinning of this tall tower. "The construction crew dug a pit seven feet deep, and during construction they kept it pumped dry of water. At the bottom of the pit they placed a wood grillage of 6" by 12" timber laid in two courses, one at right angles to the other. Decay posed no problem since the wood was to rest in at least four feet of [fresh] water. The builders then laid large granite blocks, eighteen inches thick, on the grillage. On top of that they laid courses of rubble block weighing one to five tons, so as to raise the foundation an additional five feet. Each course of stone was grouted with hydraulic Portland cement. On this foundation the builders placed the base of the tower which was cut granite on the outside and rubble set [in] cement on the inside."

The light was finally exhibited October 1, 1872. The tower was painted with black and white bands in 1873 to serve as a clear daymark for mariners, and North Carolina had added another pearl to its string of classic lighthouses.

A location at Paul Gamiel's Hill near Kitty Hawk about 15 miles to the north had been considered for the new lighthouse. However, since a light had been planned for Currituck Beach by then, the Lighthouse Service employed its new concept to build lighthouses approximately 40 miles apart so a mariner picked up the next light on his bow before losing the one on his stern; thus, Bodie Island was situated in its special location that we see today. This area claimed

Continued on p. 109

The first step in the restoration process was to remove the first-order Fresnel lens so it would not be damaged during work at the lantern-room level. Eight hands, eight eyes, a line, cautious movement and concentration were required to keep the irreplaceable lens from harm while being disassembled, crated, and stored. Photo and information courtesy of Kim Fahlen of Lighthouse Lamp Shop.

Engineers of Independence

Almost as gravely as General George Washington needed trained troops to fight the British at the onset of the War for Independence in 1775, he also needed engineers to build bulwarks, roads, bridges, and ground defenses. In Washington's opinion, the country would never be truly independent until it had its own engineers to propel a country that lacked engineering knowledge and skilled military to one leading in both fields. But the colonial states had no schools for engineers; indeed, Washington's two favorite engineers were Rufus Putnam and Henry Knox, both self-educated. The general had to otherwise rely on French engineers for advice and direction. In all probability he would have turned to British engineers had the fledgling nation not been at war with England. Out of this necessity was born West Point Academy in 1802, which became a school for military training and engineering. President Thomas Jefferson

Following the Revolutionary War, President Jefferson ordered a college be started for military and engineering training—sorely needed in the new nation. Secretary of War Henry Dearborn had the task of starting West Point Academy in 1802. During that same time, Dearborn was in charge of construction at Shell Castle Island Light and the first Cape Hatteras Lighthouse. Painting courtesy of Library of Congress

Top-ranked West Point graduates became U.S. Army Corps of Engineers or Corps of Topographical Engineers, merged in 1863. His superintendent of construction gave James Hervey Simpson credit for Cape Hatteras as a "work of topographical genius." Photo courtesy of NARA

assigned Secretary of War Henry Dearborn, Revolutionary War leader and builder of Shell Castle and Cape Hatteras Lighthouses (1803), with the duty to set regulations for cadets and officially organize the academy. Among West Point's early graduates were future wartime leaders and heroes such as Robert E. Lee, George Meade, Peter C. Hains, James Hervey Simpson, Danville Ledbetter, and W. H. C. Whiting. After graduation these men blazed trails westward into unknown territories, built infrastructure, and designed and built lighthouses. Ushering in a new age of scientific technology were other West Point and Navy Institute graduates: Alexander Dallas Bache, Superintendent of Coast Survey, and brothers Richard Bache, a champion for adoption of the Fresnel lens lighting system in America, and Hartman Bache, member of the Coast Survey along with their first cousin, George Mifflin Bache. A. D. Bache would later join his close friend,

Peter Conover Hains, West Point class of 1861, graduated right into the Civil War to become a leader like dozens of his alumni. He finished up at Cape Hatteras in 1870 and moved on to Bodie Island and Currituck Beach Lighthouses. While walking the West Potomac Park Tidal Basin at cherry-blossom time, Hains' engineering is evident there also because he oversaw the design and construction. Photo courtesy of NARA

Joseph Henry, Secretary of the Smithsonian Institute and Chairman of the Lighthouse Service, as two of President Lincoln's top picks to form the National Academy of Sciences in 1863. Coast surveying served to provide mariners with up-to-date maps and provided the government with a guide for selecting new lighthouse sites. However, it was risky business and among those who lost their lives performing this service were George Mifflin Bache, who perished in a gale off Cape Hatteras on September 8, 1846, and Richard Bache, who drowned on the West Coast surveying a site for St. George's Reef Lighthouse in 1850. All four Baches were great-grandsons of Benjamin Franklin, a pioneering scientist and inventor himself. These are a few of the great minds who turned a backward and failing Lighthouse Service into the best in the world.

The tower and lantern room were encircled by a complex 2,000-piece scaffolding system to signal that restoration had begun. Photo courtesy of Courtney A. Whisler

Continued from p. 104

many lives as witnessed by keepers' children who remembered their fathers telling them that five ships wrecked while the lighthouse was being built over a fifteen-month period. In the 1872 Lighthouse Service Annual Report, a list of six unfortunate ships appears: *Muscavado*, *Marion*, *Sarah Peters*, *Baltic*, *Willie* and a sixth unidentified ship. The Lighthouse Service wanted to make the point that for the value of cargo lost, estimated at $133,000, that the expense of the lighthouse construction, about $140,000, would "pay for itself."

For unknown reasons other than a tight economy in 1872, only one keepers' house was built for three keepers and an assistant and their families. The house design had two sides that mirrored one another. Before the National Park Service took over the property, each half had its own entrance and stairway to the second floor. Downstairs, each side housed a kitchen, office/sitting area, and a living room. On either side of each keeper's stairway were two bedrooms and a small area for a bathroom, although it was never used for such. Each keeper's bedroom faced the lighthouse so he could keep an eye on the light at all times.

Bodie Island Today

After nearly 140 years of service, the Bodie Island Lighthouse, like hundreds of other American lighthouses, needs continued restoration. While global satellite positioning has taken over these gentle giants' duties, local, state, and federal entities as well as nonprofit groups have become caretakers of our lighthouses. Restoration requires experienced contractors and expenses are large, but the rewards are tremendous. The NPS is striving to keep this light shining and allow visitors to experience the beautiful panoramic view from the top. The 1878 Bodie Island Life-Saving Station, originally called "Tommy's Hummock," and the 1925 Bodie Island Coast Guard Station have been moved from the edge of the ocean to the entrance of the light station.

BODIE ISLAND LIGHTHOUSE
Location: 4 miles north of Oregon Inlet
Nearest town: Nags Head
Built: 1872
Tower height: 167.5 feet
Elevation of focal plane: 150 feet
Number of steps: 214
Building material: Brick, cast iron, stone
Design/paint scheme: Alternating white and black horizontal bands
Optic: Fresnel lens (first-order); range of visibility, 19 nautical miles
Status: Active
Access: Tower not open for climbing
Owner/manager: National Park Service
For more information:
    Cape Hatteras National Seashore
    1401 National Park Drive
    Manteo, NC 27954
    www.nps.gov/caha/historyculture/bodie-island-light-station.htm

    Outer Banks Lighthouse Society
    P.O. Box 1005
    Morehead City, NC 28557
    www.outerbankslighthousesociety.org

As the sun sets at the end of another day at Bodie Island, the lighthouse comes to life.

Sightseers to the light station, virtually untouched by twenty-first century intrusions, are invited to walk the grounds at any time and take the easy trek along the Bodie Island Dike trail, adjacent to the lighthouse property. Some of the estuarine area, once managed by the Bodie Island Hunt Club, was dammed and formed a freshwater pond. A diverse abundance of animals and birds inhabit the pristine area. Sunrise and sunset create chameleon-like skies; the opening and closing of a day at Bodie Island are when the sun casts brilliant firelight hues on the trees, sky, and water.

CHAPTER SIX

Currituck Beach: In a New Light

The feeling of quietude within the Currituck Beach Lighthouse complex is quickened by undertones of excitement as visitors anticipate climbing all the way up the towering lighthouse's spiral stairs and taking in an unforgettable panoramic view. This historic northern Outer Banks site is steeped in history, architecture, romance, and mystery. Besides offering visitors a tower climb that serves as an aerobic workout, the Currituck Beach Light Station is part of an authentic living-history district. Outer Banks Conservationists, Inc., nonprofit, permanent stewards of the light station, have rewritten history with one of the most successful restorations in America. The 1875 light station has been returned to its glory days; furthermore, plans continue to secure the light station its deserved, protected place amidst modern resort development.

Nestled amidst these modern intrusions, this lighthouse takes a visitor back to a simpler time over 135 years ago. This nineteenth-century tower boasts outstanding brickwork, superior ironwork, and a lantern room that holds a beautiful first-order Fresnel lens, one of the few original lenses still operating in an American lighthouse. Transcending the present, the scene becomes that of a small fishing village where everyone lived in tune with nature, in which tides were the only clocks, and where every activity was in sync with the sea and weather.

Approximately 100,000 visitors seek out the Currituck Lighthouse every year. From the top, a panoramic view that sweeps from Atlantic Ocean to Currituck Sound is the reward for making the climb. The vantage point provides a remarkable view of the lighthouse property below as well as the Whalehead Club and historic Corolla Village, including the Kill Devil Hills Life-Saving Station, one-room schoolhouse, and chapel.

1875	**(December 1)** Currituck Beach Light first-order Fresnel lens illuminated.
1876	The Victorian "stick style" keepers' house completed; three keepers and their families share the duplex.
1886	Earthquake shakes lighthouse.
1920s	An 1880s dwelling moved from Long Point Light Station (depot) to light station as smaller keeper's residence.
1939	Light automated under U.S. Coast Guard (USCG) control and houses abandoned.
1952	Property surrounding lighthouse turned over to N.C. Wildlife Resources Commission for muskrat research.
1973	Light Station listed on National Register of Historic Places.
1980	**(January)** Outer Banks Conservationists (OBC) formed; OBC signs lease with State of North Carolina to begin phased restoration; a consortium of OBC, N.C. Dept. of Cultural Resources, U.S. government, and N.C. Wildlife Property successfully applies to obtain entire 30.58-acre tract on the National Register of Historic Places (National Register application filed 1973, pre-OBC, by Division of Archives and History in Raleigh).
1990	OBC negotiates with USCG to open lighthouse to public climbing.
1991	Smaller keeper's house stabilized with help of N.C. Dept. of Cultural Resources.
1995	Currituck Beach Light Station restoration considered complete in revival of one of state's most remarkable maritime resources.
1999	Reunion held for Currituck Beach Lighthouse keepers' descendants; oral histories and historic photographs collected.
2003	**(October)** OBC, Inc. is awarded ownership of the Currituck Beach Lighthouse pursuant to the National Lighthouse Preservation Act of 2000.
2011	OBC continues restoration of all parts of light station.

Plans for American lighthouse construction came to an abrupt halt during the War Between the States. Following the war, the Lighthouse Service resumed its building plan for tall coastal towers along the shoal-studded barrier islands that had begun before hostilities at Cape Lookout in 1859. After completing Cape Hatteras and replacing the war-ravaged Bodie Island Light (then known as Body's Island), a lofty tower was planned at a new site at Currituck Beach. The community had been formerly known by various names including Poyner's Hill, Jones Hill, and Whalehead; later, in 1895, the town officially became Corolla, meaning the petals of a flower, with the building of a post office. The name Currituck was derived from an Indian term "Carotank," meaning land of the wild geese. Much of the Outer Banks are on the American flyway where, before overhunting occurred, enormous flocks of geese once used the area as a migratory stopover for rest and feeding. The lighthouse assumed the name reference and became Currituck Beach.

SWIFTNESS REQUESTED

In 1873, there was a sense of congressional urgency to complete this lighthouse due to numerous wrecks on the shoals off Currituck Beach. A lighthouse at Currituck Beach had been requested as early as 1854. In a letter from February 16, 1855, Henri Lepaute, maker of Fresnel lenses in Paris, France, acknowledged an order for an illuminating apparatus for

CURRITUCK BEACH LIGHTHOUSE
Location: Currituck Sound
Nearest town: Corolla
Built: 1875
Tower height: 163 feet
Elevation of focal plane: 158 feet
Number of steps: 214
Building material: Brick
Design/paint scheme: Unpainted red brick
Optic: Fresnel lens (first-order); range of visibility, 19 nautical miles
Status: Active
Access: Seasonally open for climbing
Owner/manager: Beacon operated by U.S. Coast Guard; lighthouse and property owned by Outer Banks Conservationists
For more information:
Outer Banks Conservationists
P.O. Box 58/ 1101 Corolla Village Road
Corolla, NC 27929
(252) 453-8152
www.currituckbeachlight.com
currituckbeachlighthouse@gmail.com

Currituck Lighthouse. In a second letter dated September 12, 1855, Lepaute stated that a "2nd order [Fresnel lens] to be shipped per '*Mountaneer*'" and, in a subsequent letter that same day, sent an invoice for the lens. On April 4, 1856, Inspector Case at the Stanton Island Lighthouse Depot, New York, recorded that the lens intended for Currituck would be forwarded to Key West, Florida. Construction plans had shifted to a replacement light at Bodie Island that would hold a third-order lens. Since a light had always been considered a necessity at Bodie Island, a second tower was planned and built in

The small structure to the right of the keepers' house is a cistern. Rain water was gathered from roof runoff and directed through pipes to a cistern on either side of the house to provide fresh water for keepers' families. This technique of water storage was standard for all American lighthouses until the mid-twentieth century.

1858 and 1859, leaving plans for the Currituck Beach Lighthouse once again on the drawing board. Certainly the Board intended to go ahead with the new lighthouse at Currituck Beach, but the War Between the States held these building plans hostage; moreover, the new Bodie Island Lighthouse became a fallen soldier when it was destroyed by Confederates in 1861. Currituck would once again have to wait to become a priority for construction.

New lighthouses were being planned at Bodie Island and Currituck Beach by 1870. After debating specific sites, Congress decided in favor of rebuilding near the former Bodie Island location, and plans for a Currituck Beach tower were made for a site approximately 40 miles to the north.

In an intense move to build a light, Fifth District engineer Peter C. Hains wrote two letters dated March and April 1873 requesting permission to advertise for and to complete proposals for the ironwork. These letters are just prior to and simultaneous with a letter asking for assistance from the U.S. District Attorney in investigating titles of owners of land for the proposed site. Hains was not waiting around for a clear deed before getting construction bids and materials lined up. He had already completed boring samples in the area to identify the type of soil that he would be encountering, and, therefore, what kind of foundation was needed. When one of the two tracts of land in consideration was approved July 30, 1873, Hains was already moving ahead with plans to get this tower reaching skyward and beaming seaward.

When construction of the Currituck Beach Lighthouse began, there must have been a flurry of activity that awakened the sleepy fishing village. Temporary quarters for workmen, a carpenter's shop, blacksmith's shop, and cement shed were created. A pier at Church's Island was built for landing materials and a tramway, or railway, was put in place to carry these materials to the site. A parade of men and machinery announced to the community that a lighthouse was finally arriving. On May 29, 1874, expressing his logical validation for

The graceful 214 cast-iron steps lead to the lantern room. Each landing is attached to the inner brick wall of the tower to provide stability and strength to the entire stair system.

Each level of the tower has a window on alternating sides. In an age before electricity, natural sunlight flooded into the lighthouse; additionally, keepers could keep a watch on the light station, vessels at sea or in the sound, and weather conditions.

building this lighthouse, Hains wrote Lighthouse Service Board members the names of ships that had wrecked in the vicinity over a twenty-year period to bear witness that the expense of lost ships, lives, and cargoes far outweighed the expense of the lighthouse estimated at $178,000.

A tremendous amount of lighthouse work was ongoing along the state's coast during this time. Bodie Island had just been completed and leftover bricks were shipped to Cape Lookout to build a new keepers' quarters. Distinguishing daymarks were painted in black and white "checkers" on Cape Lookout, spirals on Cape Hatteras, and bands on Bodie Island in 1873. This allowed Currituck Beach to wear its natural red brick color as its daymark. Lighted December 1, 1875, the Currituck Beach Lighthouse was the last tall, coastal light to be built by the Lighthouse Service along the Outer Banks of North Carolina. With its first-order Fresnel lens, it shed light on the last dark stretch of featureless shoreline between Cape Henry and Bodie Island for the first time in history. It joined a network of navigational aids on the coast and in the sounds as well as rivers and harbor entrances.

A Gem Is Added to the Coast

Looking at the Currituck Beach Lighthouse and its accompanying keepers' quarters, it is obvious that architects and builders were interested in more than just bricks and mortar. The architectural drawings for the Currituck Beach Light were the same as used at Bodie Island, however there are flairs within its details not found in other North Carolina lighthouses.

Dexter Stetson was assigned to this job, since he came to the Currituck project after having successfully completed Cape Hatteras and Bodie Island. Archived letters and letter indexes indicate that he had been part of the

Keepers' Children's Memories

Homer Treadwell Austin Sr. (1881–1949) served at several North Carolina light stations including Cape Hatteras, Bodie Island, and Currituck Beach Lighthouse. He also served at Middle Ground (Newport News) and Thomas Point, both Chesapeake Bay lights. He married his lovely Orphia (Midgett) in June 1907. Later that same year, he started his long career with the Lighthouse Service. Homer and Orphia had a large family of eight children. Two of his daughters shared memories of their childhood lighthouse days and their keeper-father.

Maretta "Ret" and Mildred "Mill" were not only sisters, but fast buddies while growing up, according to Ret. The two girls were so close in age they could have been called Irish twins.

Before earning the esteemed position as first assistant at Currituck in spring 1928, Austin took two positions at Chesapeake Bay Lights. Keepers often took assignments that were far from home in order to gain the more prized and well-paying positions at the "big lights" along the North Carolina coast.

Ret told a story about staying with her dad at a "sparkplug" lighthouse, Middle Ground, in the Chesapeake Bay with her sister. These lighthouses were named for their sparkplug shape and they were located in the bay, totally surrounded by water, often a mile or several miles from land. In other words, it wasn't exactly a place to take your dog for a walk . . . or to host two young girls.

"We fished, played cards, anything we could think of," Ret recalled. "And often we got bored, so we made up lots of games. Once we sneaked my father's hammer out on the deck. We found some slate and broke it up into little pieces so we could play 'tiddly winks.' Oh, no! Daddy was not happy! But he was such an understanding parent, and he didn't punish us."

Mill recalled, "Living at the Currituck Light were some of the happiest days of my life. I used to drive our mother to Virginia Beach to grocery shop. I was probably too young to be at the wheel of an automobile, but with no police patrol and riding the wash [low tide], one did not have to be concerned with speeding or getting a ticket."

Mill is the sister that Ret called the "bold one. She'd do anything!" Ret laughed. "We had such great areas to explore on our own. Daddy took care of the lighthouse and Mama took care of everything else."

Keepers, visitors, children, and family pets have walked this walkway to and from the tower and all around the light station. It is one of the "flairs" of this historic site's design that gives it a unique personality amongst all other N.C. lighthouses.

As the sun sets across Currituck Sound, the first-order Fresnel lens is automatically turned on by a photoelectric cell.

genius behind building these fine lighthouse projects. After completing Bodie Island, he requested a leave of absence January 16, 1873, due to his wife's illness; she would die in 1874. He likely returned quickly because a letter dated just five days later in January from the Lighthouse Service Board named Stetson "Superintendent Of Construction of the Currituck Beach light in NC." According to Lighthouse Service documents, Stetson left the Currituck project March 22, 1875, handing his duties over to J. W. Lewis when construction was nearing conclusion. Stetson was reassigned to other projects until his retirement in 1886.

The foundation was similar to that at Cape Hatteras and Bodie Island; the wooden grillage was probably filled with Portland cement that has been found in other coastal lighthouses of this period. This was topped by rubble stone granite and would prove a sturdy foundation for Currituck.

The lighthouse received a more spacious oil room entryway, elliptical brick paths connecting all parts of the light station, and an added gem: the two-and-one-half-story double keepers' quarters. The keepers' house is a Victorian "stick style" dwelling, which was constructed from pre-cut labeled materials that were shipped by barge and assembled on site starting in November 1875.

"Stick style" architecture is also known as Carpenter Gothic of the early 1800s and revived as Renaissance Gothic in the late 1800s with fine wood embellishments and dramatic, elegant details including wooden finials at the gable ends. The keepers' dwelling was built as a duplex; each side mirrored the other. The downstairs of each house contains three large rooms with fireplaces in each and each side had an attached front porch. A cistern at each end of the house collected rain water as the only source of fresh water. The keepers' house and tower were connected by double walkways, two separate yards, and a fence that ran down the middle to denote each keeper's area. Although it was meant to house two keepers and their families, the principal keeper had half of the house and two assistants and their families shared one side of the duplex for several years. When needed, the third floor was also used as a living area to ease overcrowding.

NEARING COMPLETION

Fifth District engineer Harwood took over the Currituck Beach Lighthouse project from Hains in summer 1874. Hains designed and helped at both the Morris Island and St. Augustine Lighthouses, of the same design that Hains did for Currituck Beach and Bodie Island Lighthouses. Through indexed letters, the daily details of completing the light station unfold. Harwood ordered the first-order lighting apparatus August 21, 1875, and just four days later the lens was on its way from the Lighthouse Depot in Tompkinsville, New York (Staten Island). The foreman of the Lamp Shop at the Lighthouse Depot had discovered a damaged prism and, after being repaired, a letter from Lighthouse Depot engineer I. C. Woodruff on August 25, 1875, recorded the shipment of the

A rising winter's full moon adds warmth to a cold night in companionship with the Currituck Beach Lighthouse's first-order Fresnel lens and its 1,000-watt electric bulb.

Note the absence of trees and other foliage that allows a clear view of the Currituck Beach Light Station in this 1883 Bamber photograph. It is the only coastal lighthouse site in North Carolina where just one tower was erected. Photo courtesy of Outer Banks History Center

lens to Harwood. He wrote a proposed Notice to Mariners for lighting the new lens, but he wrote another letter September 16, 1875, having found an error.

The project was drawing to a close. Harwood suggested a head keeper October 1, 1875. One week later, other keepers and salaries were announced in two letters by Fifth District Inspector Baker. A metallic guide roller for the rotating red bulls-eye panels was requested that same day and was quickly shipped. Inspector Baker requested coal and wood for the keepers on October 18. Curtain rollers were requested December 13 to hold the protective lantern room curtains that, when drawn closed during the day, shielded the Fresnel lens from damaging heat and sunlight as well as provided a cooler working area for keepers. Directives in "Instructions to Employees of the Lighthouse Service, 1881" detail these keepers' duties; further, keepers' children were instructed in these details by their keeper-fathers during the early twentieth century. Cleaning glass storm panes, polishing brass, cleaning the crown crystal prisms of the lens, and keeping every speck of dust off any surfaces in the lantern room required considerable physical labor. Help from the young ones was always welcome.

Supplies for keepers were sent by Lighthouse Service tenders to keep every part of the lighthouse in top condition. A keeper protected a Fresnel lens with paternal passion because the lens magnified light emitted from a lamp at its center to yield an intense beam of light for mariners. And, should the light be out for any reason, a keeper's job was at risk. Harwood requested an emergency, or extra, oil-burning wick "Funck" lamp.

The light station was coming to life, and on the evening of Wednesday, December 1, 1875, at long last, mariners saw a light to help them safely navigate this dangerous area.

The lighthouse tower, and a grand one it is, stands approximately 163 feet tall; its focal plane, the center of the lens where light is emitted, is at 158 feet. Its first-order Fresnel lens originally carried a "fixed varied [red] revolving flash" every ninety seconds, which means a white beam shone steadily and was broken by a red flash. A red-glass panel revolved on chariot wheels outside the big lens and was turned by a clockwork mechanism driven by a suspended weight beneath the lantern. A keeper opened an enclosed area within the pedestal on which the huge lens and red panel rested and cranked the weight up by hand every two and a half hours. Its flame was held by a lamp consisting of five concentric wicks. The flash characteristic of a fixed-white light accompanied by a red flash varied several times over the years. The red warning flash was produced by glass that was manufactured by adding gold to render it ruby colored. The red sector was eventually removed, likely in 1939 when the U.S. Coast Guard automated the light.

Approximately one million bricks comprise the lighthouse walls that are 5 feet, 8 inches thick at the base and taper to 3 feet thick at the parapet under the lantern room. As with the other tall coastal lights, vertical windows were spaced along the spiral stairs that looked out onto the Atlantic Ocean and Currituck Sound. These windows not only provided natural light along the stairwell during an era before electricity but also allowed a keeper to observe from a birds-eye view any approaching ships. During the late 1800s, keepers helped watch for distressed ships and relayed any news to the nearby Jones Hill Life-Saving Station.

The dignified red-brick lighthouse has two brick anterooms at the base, one on each side of the entryway. One was used as an office and general work area, and another was built to accommodate barrels of oil. Each was complete with a fireplace and a heavy wooden door that could be closed for warmth; the doors opened into a central passageway that led to the spiral stairs. This made for a comfortable working environment at ground level although keepers did not live in the lighthouse. In 1896, oil was stored outside the lighthouse for fire-safety reasons.

A wreath of netting around the lantern room area was added for several years to catch waterfowl that were blinded by the light. Sometimes entire

care of the lighthouse and Grandmother Orphia ran the household and took care of a passel of kids. In this way, caring for a lighthouse was a family affair with duties assigned to everyone and strict schedules to adhere to. In the 1881 handbook given each keeper and his assistant, there are 204 individual rules listed; not following any of these rules meant dismissal.

Four generations later in 1978, Wilson, who was an architect, saw his great-grandfather's forsaken and windowless keepers' home and dared to dream of returning it to its former glory. Wilson, along with William Parker, Anne Bahr, Meile Rockefeller, and Lee Salet, formed a group for the purpose of restoration and preservation of the light station called the Outer Banks Conservationists, Inc (OBC).

Lighthouse Ownership, No "Light" Job

The light station is located on a 30.58-acre site deeded by the federal government to the state in 1952 for muskrat research and other public recreational purposes. Responsibility for the tract, with the exception of the lighthouse that was still owned then by the Coast Guard, was vested in the North Carolina Wildlife Resources Commission. When Wilson offered to restore the house and attend to cleaning up the grounds, the budget-strapped Resources Commission found this a win-win situation. A detailed restoration and maintenance proposal from OBC was approved by the Resources Commission eighteen months later and a fifty-year lease for the property was handled by the Department of Cultural Resources.

With that lease in 1980, OBC took on the redoubtable task of restoring the keepers' house, of which only three others of its kind were built in America, earning it architectural significance and an honored place on the National Register of Historic Places. It is a two-and-a-half-story Victorian "stick style" dwelling that was constructed from pre-cut and labeled materials that were shipped via barge by the Lighthouse Service and assembled on site. Its four grand chimneys and beautiful woodwork throughout the house are just a few of the details that made this house a grand work of art. All restoration work at the light station must be done according to the U.S. Secretary of the Interior's Standards for Historic Preservation as well as guidelines of the North Carolina Secretary of Cultural Resources. It was not until years later that OBC added the lighthouse to its restoration plans. As tourism grew with the completion of NC Highway 12 through Duck to Corolla, visitors to the grounds found the spruced-up lighthouse grounds intriguing. Thus, getting the tower ready for public access seemed the natural thing to do and OBC proceeded with the plan—no small job.

Complete restoration has brought the keepers' house back to its original glory, thanks to the perseverance and care by its stewards, Outer Banks Conservationists, Inc. It is the only one surviving of three keepers' houses built of this Victorian "stick style" in America. Once considered an eyesore and asked to be razed by the county, it is now a beautiful addition to the historic district. The house arrived in a "kit" with pre-cut and numbered timber and other labeled materials for assembly. At times, three families shared the house, making it a lively scene with children all about. The two sides of the house mirror one another with a third floor that was used when extra living space was needed. Photos courtesy of The Outer Banks Conservationists, Inc.

We shall never forget our first climb to the lantern room atop the Cape Lookout Lighthouse, courtesy of superintendent Bob Vogel. Even more important, Bob helped us find documents confirming that Capt. William H. C. Whiting supervised the design and construction of the Cape Lookout Lighthouse when he was still a member of the esteemed U.S. Army Corps of Engineers.

In Wilmington, Cathy Boettcher and her staff at the Lower Cape Fear Historical Society offered a gold mine of information about the Cape Fear River. Ray Flowers, historic interpreter at Fort Fisher Historic Site, helped us explore the subject of the mound battery and of the signal lights used by Confederate blockade runners.

Chris Fonvielle of the University of North Carolina at Wilmington and author of *The Wilmington Campaign* provided insights and information about the Civil War years and our mutual hero, Major General Whiting, whose engineering skills were put to use in defending the last port open to Confederate blockade runners. Another source of information was Beverly Tetteron, Special Collections librarian at the New Hanover County Library in Wilmington.

On the south side of the Cape Fear River, we thank Mary Strickland, manager of the North Carolina Maritime Museum at Southport, who was most helpful and knowledgeable about lighthouses of the area. Also Elbert Felton of the N.C. Division of Tourism, Film, and Sports Development and Jim A. Bartley, historic site manager at Brunswick Town. At Bald Head Island, Jane Oakley and the Old Baldy Foundation deserve everyone's thanks for their work in preserving the 1817 Old Baldy Lighthouse, a landmark that is kept open to the public.

At Currituck Beach Light Station in Corolla, our appreciation goes to John Wilson, William Parker, site manager Meghan Agresto, and the Outer Banks Conservationists, the nonprofit preservation organization that has brought this famous lighthouse back to life and achieved one of the best restorations in America.

In addition to the people within North Carolina, many from outside the state also contributed to this book. Ray Jones, author of this book's foreword and our co-author for nearly a dozen lighthouse books, has shared our trips, the wonder of discovering America's lighthouses, and the exciting stories of the men and women who devoted their lives' work to lighting our coast. Rick Polad, who has also been with us for much of the journey, helped search and comment on the sea of words that abounds around lighthouses. Lighthouse historian Jim Claflin provided not only information, but in many cases the actual documents. Thanks also to lighthouse historian Candace Clifford, whose 1994 book, *Inventory of Historic Light Stations*, is the standard in the field.

Thomas A. Tag, Fresnel lens expert, answered dozens of our questions. He generously shared his years of study both at home and abroad to deepen our understanding and respect for these irreplaceable, revolutionary optics.

There are so many others whose assistance we wish to acknowledge: Brent Westwood, Laura Stokes, Marie Harris, Marie's daughter Thelma Margaret, Margaret Ann Gillikin, Dorothy Willis, and Dorothy's daughter Zina. Also, John Gaskill and Marilyn Austin Meads, children of the last lighthouse keepers at Bodie Island and Rany Jennette, son of the last keeper at Cape Hatteras. It was a privilege to work with all of these fine people. We thank them for trusting us to interview them multiple times and copy their priceless photographs.

Finally, we thank Globe Pequot Press for the opportunity to create this new edition and editorial director Erin Turner and Ellen Urban for their guidance.

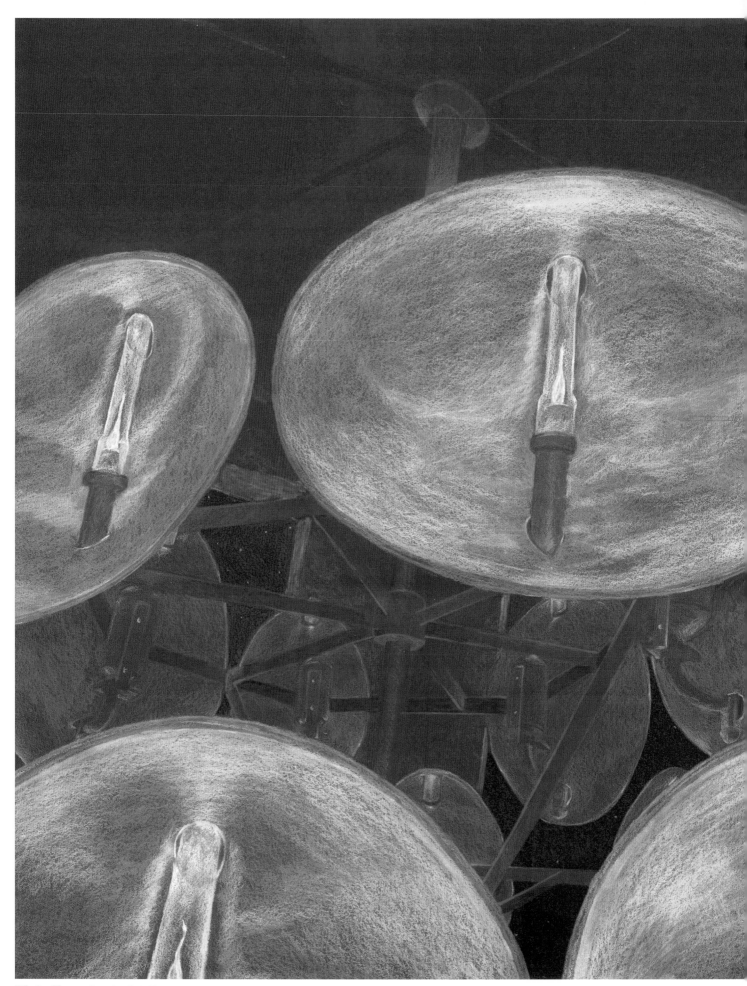

Whale oil lamps Drawing by Mike Litwin

APPENDIX: NORTH CAROLINA LIGHT LIST

A comprehensive summary of North Carolina lighthouses and lightships, based on the U.S. Lighthouse Service's annual Light List, follows.

1733 Beacon Island Lights. A pair of whale-oil lamps, probably mounted on posts, was used to mark the channel through Ocracoke Inlet. They are the first recorded aids to navigation in North Carolina, appearing on Edward Moseley's 1733 "A New and Correct Map of the Province of North Carolina."

1794   First Bald Head Island Lighthouse. Considered North Carolina's first lighthouse and also known as Cape Fear Lighthouse, it was built at the entrance to the Cape Fear River. The state began its construction in 1784, using a duty on cargo going through river ports, but the U.S. Lighthouse Service completed it. It was lost to erosion in 1813.

Sketch of the Currituck Beach Lighthouse from The Daily Graphic, *New York, Feb. 2, 1878.*

1803 First Cape Hatteras Lighthouse. Built by Revolutionary War hero Henry Dearborn, the 90-foot tower was one of the early Federal octagonal light-houses built between 1792 and 1817. President Thomas Jefferson appointed its first keeper, Adam Gaskins, in 1802. A pan of whale oil with multiple "floating" wicks provided the lights, but it was too weak to be seen where it was needed, beyond Diamond Shoals. The tower was heightened to 150 feet and painted in 1854. Replaced in 1870, it was later destroyed as surplus.

1803 (circa) Shell Castle Island Lighthouse. Constructed by Henry Dearborn on an islet also known as Old Rock Island, it was the first lighthouse to mark Ocracoke Inlet. A fire caused by lightning destroyed it in 1818.

Sketch of the Currituck Beach Lighthouse from The Daily Graphic, *New York, Feb. 2, 1878.*

1812 First Cape Lookout Lighthouse. A 93-foot brick tower covered with wood and painted red and white, it was once described as looking from a distance like a "ship of war with her sails clewed up." The beacon's thirteen oil lamps put off a weak and fitful light that mariners complained was nearly impossible to find. Rebel commandos blew it up in 1864.

1816 First Federal Point Lighthouse. Located in an area that's now part of Fort Fisher State Park, this small lighthouse was equipped with eight whale-oil lamps and positioned to illuminate the entrance to New Inlet. It burned in 1836.

1817–1818 Second Bald Head Island Lighthouse ("Old Baldy"). The oldest of North Carolina's surviving lighthouses, it remained in active service, off and on, until 1958 and now is an historic site. Early light lists refer to it as the Cape Fear Lighthouse.

1823 Ocracoke Lighthouse. North Carolina's oldest lighthouse still in use, its beacon has been in continuous operation except for a short time during the Civil War when Confederates removed its Fresnel lens. Built by Noah Porter of Massachusetts, it replaced the burned Shell Castle Island Light.

1824 Cape Hatteras Lightship. Stationed at the outer edge of Diamond Shoals off Cape Hatteras, the vessel often lost its anchorage during severe storms and was finally removed in 1827 after beaching on Ocracoke. No lightships were successfully anchored here again until 1897.

1825 Long Shoal Light-Vessel. These smaller versions of lightships, designed for inland waters, were placed in North Carolina sounds between 1825 and 1845. This straw-colored vessel marked the shoal across northern Pamlico Sound.

1826 Royal Shoal Light-Vessel. This lead-colored vessel was anchored 9 miles from the Ocracoke Lighthouse at the southwest point of Royal Shoals in Pamlico Sound.

1826 Wade's Point Light-Vessel. Stationed on the west side of the entrance to the Pasquotank River in Albemarle Sound, this light marked the way to Elizabeth City.

1827 Nine-Foot Shoal Light-Vessel. Placed about 4 miles northwest of Ocracoke Lighthouse, this white vessel marked the northeast side of Royal Shoal in Pamlico Sound.

1828 Neuse River Light-Vessel. This lead-colored vessel was anchored off March Point and marked the Neuse River entrance from Pamlico Sound.

1828 (circa) Pamlico Point Lighthouse. A white-frame octagonal structure that carried its light 37 feet above the water, it marked the channel out from Pamlico Point on the south side of the Pamlico River. Its original ten whale-oil lamps were replaced in 1856 with a fifth-order Fresnel lens. Earlier lights like Pamlico Point were about 1,000 square feet of living/working space and appeared as if cottages on stilts. Later these sound lights would take on either a hexagonal design or rectangular cottage style, more cost efficient to build and maintain.

1831 Brant Island Shoal Light-Vessel. This was the first light to mark the point of the shoal in southern Pamlico Sound.

1823 Ocracoke Light

1835 Roanoke Island Light-Vessel. Also called Croatan Light-Vessel, this lead-colored vessel marked the channel between Pamlico and Albemarle Sounds.

1835 Roanoke River Light-Vessel. Stationed in Albemarle Sound, this light marked the entrance to the Roanoke River.

1836 Harbor Island Light-Vessel. Also called the Harkers Island Light-Vessel, this red-painted ship on the bar marked the channel between Pamlico and Core Sounds.

1838 Second Federal Point Lighthouse. A brick tower erected to mark New Inlet, it was demolished by Confederate soldiers in 1861 to give them a clear range of fire on Union forces. The tower's bricks were used in the construction of Fort Fisher; the keeper's house became the fort's headquarters.

1845 Wade's Point Light-Vessel. This yellow, seventy-six-ton lightship took over watch here, anchored on the west side of the Pasquotank River and marking passage from Albemarle Sound.

1847–1848 First Bodie Island Lighthouse. The first of three lights established here (and originally called Body's Island Lighthouse), the 57-foot white tower had a short and infamous life. Built without a foundation to save on construction costs, it began to lean shortly after being put into service and was abandoned in 1858.

1849 Oak Island Range Lights. This pair of brick towers on Oak Island guided ships over the bar into the Cape Fear River. The rear tower was 37 feet tall, the front one 27 feet; both were equipped with fifth-order Fresnel lenses. It's possible the front light was mounted on rails so it could be moved as the Cape Fear River channel changed.

1849 Campbell's Island Lighthouse. One of a series of lights used to guide ships up the Cape Fear River to Wilmington. Its sixth-order Fresnel lens was placed on the roof of the keepers' house.

1849 Orton Point Range Lights. Located near Orton Plantation on the Cape Fear River, these beacons were built from the same plans as the Price's Creek Lights.

1850 Price's Creek Range Lights Drawing by Brent Westwood

1850 Price's Creek Range Lights. The Cape Fear River range lights were virtually all destroyed during the Civil War, but a relic of this installation survives. The brick tower, missing its lantern, stands on the west bank of the river near the state ferry dock at Southport. The light was used as a Confederate signal station in 1864 and 1865 to give blockade-running ships information about the position of Union ships.

1851 Brant Island Shoal Light-Vessel. This heavy, straw-colored ship took up station in southern Pamlico Sound to mark Brant Island and the shoal.

1851 Horse-Shoe Shoal Light-Vessel. Positioned to light Ocracoke Inlet, it later served as a range light in combination with the Beacon Island Light.

1853 Beacon Island Lighthouse. This light, inside the Ocracoke Inlet channel, was a brick keepers' house with a lantern room on the roof and served as a range light with a light vessel to mark the channel. Originally equipped with 10 whale-oil lamps visible 11 miles, it was later upgraded with a sixth-order Fresnel lens. A hurricane submerged Beacon Island in 1933.

1854 Frying Pan Lightship. The anchoring of this lightship at the outer end of Frying Pan Shoals launched a coastal watch system that continued for more than a century. It was painted yellow with the words "Frying Pan" in black on both sides.

1855 Wade's Point Lighthouse. Spiderlike cottage-style hexagonal screw-pile lighthouses were established throughout North Carolina sounds to take the place of light vessels. This one, equipped with a fifth-order Fresnel lens, marked the channel into the Pasquotank River and Elizabeth City docks. The screw-piles were phased out in the 1950s.

1855 Bogue Banks Beacon Lights. This set of beacons at Fort Macon in Beaufort Harbor Inlet (formerly Old Topsail Inlet) marked the channel for this busy port. The main light was a brick 50-foot tower with a fourth-order Fresnel lens; the other, a 30-foot wood platform with a sixth-order lens. Removed by Confederate soldiers during the Civil War, they were not rebuilt.

1855 Upper Jetty Range Lights. This installation was the last in the system of lights that marked the winding Cape Fear River channel to the Wilmington docks.

1856 Cape Hatteras Beacon Light. This modest, 20-foot-tall wooden lighthouse stood 27 feet above sea level and was situated about halfway between the first Cape Hatteras Lighthouse and the tip of Cape Point to guide local boaters into Pamlico Sound. The demure beacon was moved several times due to erosion and was lit for a final time in 1898. Replaced by a light on a nearby pole, it was also discontinued in 1905.

1857 Northwest Point Royal Shoal Lighthouse. Situated 9 miles from the Ocracoke Lighthouse, this octagonal screw-pile sat in 6 feet of water and was equipped with a fourth-order Fresnel lens.

1857 Roanoke Marshes Lighthouse. This screw-pile lighthouse replaced the light-vessel that had marked the south entrance to the channel between Pamlico and Albemarle Sounds.

1859 Second Bodie Island Lighthouse. Designed by Captain Lorenzo Sitgreaves of the U.S. Army Corps of Topographical Engineers, this lighthouse was in service only two years. Confederate troops destroyed it to prevent its being helpful to Union forces preparing an attack on Roanoke Island.

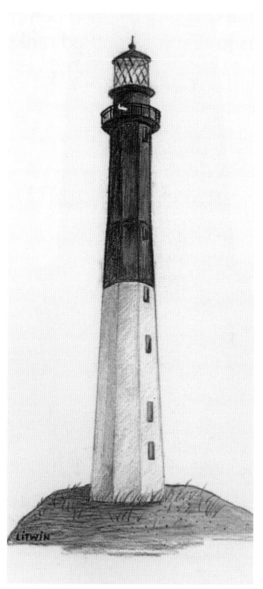

1854 First Cape Hatteras Lighthouse after it had been heightened to 150 feet Drawing by Mike Litwin

1859 Cape Lookout Lighthouse. A model for the other tall coastal lighthouses built in North Carolina in the nineteenth century, this 163-foot-tall brick tower remains in service today. Capt. W. H. C. Whiting, Chief Engineer Sixth District U.S. Army Corps of Engineers supervised its design and construction. Its first-order Fresnel lens was replaced with a modern optic in 1967.

1860 Croatan Lighthouse. Also known as Caroon's Point Lighthouse, this square screw-pile structure marked the channel from Albemarle Sound into Croatan Sound. It was blown up in 1864 by a Confederate raiding party from the CSS *Albemarle* and the keeper taken prisoner.

1862 Neuse River Lighthouse. This square screw-pile structure was situated in 5 feet of water where the Neuse River joins Pamlico Sound. The lighthouse was under construction when the Civil War began and was finished after Union forces took control of the area early in the war. It was an important guide to the port of New Bern, which was a critical supply depot for Union armies.

1866 Second Croatan Lighthouse. Built as a replacement for the screw-pile destroyed by Confederates in 1864, the square cottage-style lighthouse featured green shutters and a brown roof. Also known as Caroon's Point, Roanoke Island, and Mashoes Creek, it marked the entrance to Croatan Sound from Albemarle Sound.

1866 First Roanoke River Lighthouse. This square screw-pile lighthouse stood in 7 feet of water in Albemarle Sound near the entrance to the Roanoke River. Its pilings were painted red, the house white, and it displayed a red light from a fourth-order Fresnel lens.

1866 Third Federal Point Lighthouse. A marker for New Inlet leading into the Cape Fear River, this light replaced the lighthouse destroyed during the Civil War. The 45-foot-tall white, two-story house surmounted by a lantern room was located near the ruins of Fort Fisher. Discontinued when the Army

Corps of Engineers purposely closed New Inlet a decade later in 1880, it burned down in 1881.

1866 Oak Island Range Lights. These range lights were square at the foundation rising to wooden pyramidal structures painted white for visibility. They replaced a set of lights presumed destroyed during the Civil War.

1866 North River Lighthouse. This square screw-pile structure rested in 3½ feet of water on the shoaled bar at the entrance to North River in Albemarle Sound.

1867 Long Shoal Lighthouse. Standing in 9 feet of water in northern Pamlico Sound and equipped with a fourth-order Fresnel lens, this screw-pile replaced a light-vessel that had marked the shoal.

1867 Southwest Point Royal Shoal Lighthouse. This square, white screw-pile stood in Pamlico Sound about 8 miles from the Ocracoke Lighthouse. It was discontinued in 1880 but relit in 1887.

1867 Harbor Island Bar Lighthouse. Sitting in 6 feet of water, this cottage-style lighthouse marked the entrance to Core Sound from Pamlico Sound. It displayed a flashing red light every ten seconds.

1870 Cape Hatteras Lighthouse. The tallest brick lighthouse in North America at 198 feet, the Hatteras Light remains an active beacon. The Lighthouse Service hired Massachusetts contractor Dexter Stetson as superintendant of construction. Erosion of the beach necessitated its being moved in 1999. The lighthouse had been abandoned from 1936 to 1950, also because of erosion worries. Owned by the National Park Service, it's part of Cape Hatteras National Seashore.

1872 Third Bodie Island Lighthouse. Construction also supervised by Stetson and Peter C. Hains, the third Bodie Island Light stands about 40 miles north of Cape Hatteras and lies within Cape Hatteras National Seashore. Still an active beacon, the tower retains its original first-order Fresnel lens.

1874 Hatteras Inlet Lighthouse. A screw-pile structure also known as Oliver's Reef Light, it stood in about 7 feet of water at the entrance to Hatteras Inlet from Pamlico Sound.

1875 Currituck Beach Lighthouse. The last of the tall coastal lights built by the U.S. Lighthouse Service in North Carolina, this tower incorporated the same plans used for the 1872 Bodie Island Light; Stetson and Hains supervised construction. Its original first-order Fresnel lens is still intact and in service. The lighthouse is now owned by Outer Banks Conservationists, a nonprofit preservation organization that has restored the tower and keepers' houses.

1877 Roanoke Marshes Lighthouse. The second screw-pile lighthouse to be placed at the southern entrance of Croatan Sound, this one featured technological improvements such as a compressed-air siren fog signal.

1879 Edenton Harbor Range Lights. In contrast to traditional range lights, the front light of this installation was positioned on a pole at the end of the county wharf and, according to the official U.S. Light List, the rear light was "400 feet northward in a tree."

1880 Laurel Point Lighthouse. This hexagonal screw-pile light was distinctive in its time for having the only flashing light on Albemarle Sound.

1891 Diamond Shoals Lighthouse. The U.S. Lighthouse Service attempted to build a 148-foot-high lighthouse on the shoals off Cape Hatteras, but the effort ended in failure.

1891 Pamlico Point Lighthouse. The U.S. Lighthouse Service rebuilt this screw-pile lighthouse at the entrance to the Pamlico River leading to Washington, North Carolina.

1891 Gull Shoal Lighthouse. This white, hexagonal screw-pile lighthouse sat on pilings 44 feet above the water at the east end of Gull Shoal in Pamlico Sound.

1897 Diamond Shoal Lightship. The first lightship at this site since 1827, this vessel had the advantage of an extremely heavy mushroom anchor that kept it on station with greater success, unlike its predecessor. Several lightships served duty at this wave-swept site, but *LV 71* was the unfortunate one on duty when it was attacked and sunk by a German submarine in 1918.

1903 Cape Fear Lighthouse. One of the new steel skeleton light towers built by the U.S. Lighthouse Service, this one stood on the ocean side of Bald Head

Diamond Shoal Lightship Photo courtesy of USCG

Island and was equipped with a first-order Fresnel lens. After the Oak Island Lighthouse went into operation in 1958, this tower was destroyed.

1903 Lookout Shoals Light-Vessel. This lightship, stationed on the outer edge of Lookout Shoals, starkly illustrated the risks of the service. Five lightship crewmen, while manning the lightship's whaleboat, were accidentally run over and drowned when attempting to transfer mail to the passing steamer *City of Atlanta* in 1913. The light-vessel was replaced with a buoy during the Great Depression.

1958 Oak Island Lighthouse. One of the last lighthouses built in the United States, this modern silo-style tower remains an active beacon operated by the U.S. Coast Guard. The lighthouse property was transferred in 2003 to the Town of Caswell Beach and volunteers are provided by Friends of Oak Island.

1966 Frying Pan Shoals Light Tower. An adapted Gulf Coast oil-rig platform, this new style of water-based lighthouse replaced the *Frying Pan* lightship. The tower stands about 20 miles southeast of Oak Island, its foundation driven

293 feet into the ocean floor. An automated beacon since 1979, the tower was scheduled for demolition but has been privately purchased.

1967 Diamond Shoals Light Tower. Rising more than 100 feet above the surface of the Atlantic about 13 miles off Cape Hatteras, this oil-rig–style lighthouse also was automated in 1979 and is scheduled for demolition.

Diamond "Texas" Tower Photo courtesy of USCG

BIBLIOGRAPHY

Blunt, Edmund, and G. W. Blunt. *The American Coast Pilot*. New York: Blunt, 1842.

Branch, Paul. "Subtlety and Subterfuge: Bombing the Lights." *The Maritimes Magazine*, 28 Oct. 1986.

Bureau of Lighthouses. U.S. Lighthouse Service Bulletins, 1912–1939. Washington, D.C.: Government Printing Office.

Carr, Dawson. *Gray Phantoms of the Cape Fear: Running the Civil War Blockade*. Winston-Salem, N.C.: John F. Blair, 1998.

Chenery III, Richard L. *Old Coast Guard Stations: North Carolina*. Glen Allen, Va.: Station Books, 2000.

Childers, Lloyd D. "Leasing a Lighthouse Complex." *North Carolina Historic Preservation Office Newsletter*, Winter 1995.

Clifford, Candace. *Inventory of Historic Light Stations*. Washington, D.C.: National Park Service, 1994.

Cloud, Ellen Fulcher. *Portsmouth: The Way It Was*. Ocracoke, N.C.: Live Oak Publications, 1996.

Duffus, Kevin. *The Lost Light: The Mystery of the Missing Cape Hatteras Fresnel Lens*. Raleigh, N.C.: Looking Glass Publications, 2003.

Elizabeth, Norma, and Bruce Roberts. *Shipwrecks Disasters & Rescues of the Graveyard of the Atlantic and Cape Fear*. Morehead City, N.C.: Lighthouse Publications, 2001.

Fonvielle Jr., Chris E. *The Wilmington Campaign: Last Rays of Departing Hope*. Campbell, Calif.: Savas Publishing, 1997.

Fulcher, Susan. "Reclaiming Its Shining Past: The Restoration of the Currituck Beach Lighthouse Property." *Lighthouse News*, vol. 3. no. 2, 1997.

Gurney, Alan. *Compass: A Story of Exploration and Innovation.* New York and London: W.W. Norton & Company, 2004.

Herring, Ethel. *Cap'n Charlie and Lights of the Lower Cape Fear.* Winston-Salem, N.C.: Hunter Publishing, 1967.

Hickam Jr., Homer. *Torpedo Junction.* Annapolis, Md.: U.S. Naval Institutes Press, 1989.

Holland Jr., F. Ross. *America's Lighthouses: An Illustrated History.* New York: Dover Publications, 1981, reprint.

___. *Great American Lighthouses.* Washington, D.C.: Preservation Press, 1994.

___. *A History of the Cape Hatteras Lightstation.* Washington, D.C.: National Park Service, 1968.

___. *A Survey History of Cape Lookout National Seashore.* Washington, D.C.: U.S. Department of Interior, 1968.

Jones, Ray. *The Lighthouse Encyclopedia.* Guilford, Conn.: Globe Pequot Press, 2004.

Kochel, Kenneth G. *America's Atlantic Coast Lighthouses: A Traveler's Guide.* Clearwater, Fla.: Betken Publications, 1996. Second Edition.

Mobley, Joe. *A Ship Ashore! The U.S. Lifesavers of Coastal North Carolina.* Chapel Hill: N.C. Division of Archives and History, 1996.

Morris, Glenn. *North Carolina Beaches.* Chapel Hill: University of North Carolina Press, 1998.

National Park Service, "Historic Lighthouse Preservation Handbook." www.cr .nps.gov/maritime/handbook.htm.

O'Connor, William D. *Heroes of the Storm.* Cambridge, Mass.: Houghton Mifflin, Riverside Press, 1904.

Payne, Roger L. *Place Names of the Outer Banks.* Washington, N.C.: Thomas A. Williams Publisher, 1985.

Putnam, George R. "Beacons of the Sea: Lighting the Coast of the United States." *National Geographic*, Jan. 1913.

___. *Lighthouses and Lightships of the United States*. Boston: Houghton Mifflin, 1917.

___. *Sentinel of the Coasts: The Log of a Lighthouse Engineer*. New York: W. W. Norton, 1937.

Roberts, Bruce, and Ray Jones. *American Lighthouses*. Guilford, Conn.: Globe Pequot Press, 1994.

___. *Southern Lighthouses*. Guilford, Conn.: Globe Pequot Press, 1994.

Rowlett, Russ, and University of North Carolina. "Early Federal Octagonals, 1792–1817. www.unc.edu/~rowlett/lighthouse/types/octaganals.html.

Shelton-Roberts, Cheryl. "After 100 Years the Superb Surfmen of the Pea Island Lifesaving Station Get the Gold." *Lighthouse News*, vol. 2, no. 2, 1996.

___. "Augustin Fresnel." *Lighthouse News*, vol. 2, no. 3, 1997.

___. "Fresnel Defies Napoleon, Newton and Death to Design Revolutionary Lens." *Lighthouse News*, vol. 2, no. 3, 1996.

___. *Lighthouse Families*. Birmingham, Ala.: Crane Hill Press, 1997.

___. "Light Years Away." *Lighthouse News*, vol. 2, no. 1, 1996.

___, ed., and Sandra MacLean Clunies. *Hatteras Keepers Oral and Family Histories*. Morehead City, N.C.: Outer Banks Lighthouse Society, 2001.

___ and Bruce Roberts. *North Carolina Lighthouses*. Morehead City, N.C.: Lighthouse Publications, 2001.

Sobel, Dava. *Longitude: The True Story of a Lone Genius Who Solved the Greatest Scientific Problem of His Time*. New York: Walker and Company, 1995.

Sprunt, James. *Chronicles of the Cape Fear River 1660–1916*. Spartanburg, S.C.: Reprint Co, 1973. (original edition 1916)

Stick, David. *Bald Head: A History of Smith Island and Cape Fear*. Wendell, N.C.: Boardfoot Publishing, 1985.

_____. *Dare County: A Brief History.* Raleigh: N.C. Department of Cultural Resources, 1970.

_____. *Graveyard of the Atlantic: Shipwrecks of the North Carolina Coast.* Chapel Hill: University of North Carolina Press, 1952.

_____. *North Carolina Lighthouses.* Raleigh: N.C. Department of Cultural Resources, 1992.

_____. ed. *An Outer Banks Reader.* Chapel Hill: University of North Carolina Press, 1998.

Tag, Thomas. *From Braziers and Bougies to Xenon.* Dayton, Ohio: Self-published.

_____. "Lighting Cape Hatteras." *Lighthouse News,* vol. 5, no. 4, 1996.

Ulanski, Stan. The Gulf Stream: Tiny Plankton, Giant Bluefin, and the Amazing Story of the Powerful River in the Atlantic. Chapel Hill: The University of North Carolina Press, 2008.

U.S. Light-House Service. List of Beacons, Buoys, and Day-Marks in the Fifth Light-House District. Washington, D.C.: Government Printing Office, 1839, 1842, 1845, 1848, 1849, 1854, 1857, 1861–65, 1867, 1879, 1880, 1881, 1882, 1884, 1888, 1889, 1890, 1897, 1898, 1899, 1902, 1932.

Walker, Paul K. Engineers of Independence: A Documentary History of the Army Engineers in the American Revolution, 1775–1783. Historical Division, Office of Administrative Services, Office of the Chief of Engineers, 1988. Weiss, George. The Lighthouse Service: Its History, Activities, and Organization. Baltimore, Md.: Johns Hopkins Press, 1926.

Weiss, George. *The Lighthouse Service: Its History, Activities, and Organization.* Baltimore, Md.: Johns Hopkins Press, 1926.

Witney, Dudley. *The Lighthouse.* Boston: New York Graphic Society, 1975.

Yocum, Thomas, Bruce Roberts, and Cheryl Shelton-Roberts. *Cape Hatteras: America's Lighthouse.* Nashville, Tenn.: Cumberland House, 1999.

INDEX

ABOUT THE AUTHORS

North Carolina native and lighthouse historian Cheryl Shelton-Roberts is the editor of *Hatteras Keepers Oral and Family Histories,* a compilation of hundreds of stories from the families of Cape Hatteras Lighthouse keepers. She is also the author of *Lighthouse Families,* a touching chronicle of the lives of U.S. lighthouse keepers' families and winner of the U.S. Coast Guard's outstanding history book for 2007. Other works include *Moving Hatteras: Relocating the Cape Hatteras Light Stations to Safety* and *Cape Hatteras: America's Lighthouse.*

Nationally acclaimed photographer Bruce Roberts served as the first director of photography for *Southern Living* magazine. His lighthouse photographs have appeared in hundreds of books and magazines, including *Our State* magazine, *Time, Life, Time-Life Books, Southern Lighthouses,* and *American Lighthouses.*

In 1994, the couple co-founded the Outer Banks Lighthouse Society, an organization dedicated to the preservation of North Carolina lighthouses, the history of the brave women and men who saved countless lives from the capricious Graveyard of the Atlantic, and the history of the U.S. Lighthouse Service. Both have been awarded the prestigious "Keeper of the Light" award from the American Lighthouse Foundation for their preservation efforts, including the part they played in the successful 1999 move of the Cape Hatteras Lighthouse to safer ground. They live in Morehead City, North Carolina.